Rhythm & Fire

Advance Praise

"They say never meet your idol, but I'm grateful I met mine. Ralph became a brother, a mentor, a guiding light. Earth, Wind & Fire lives in the DNA of my music and so many others. This book will inspire lives for generations to come."

—Kizzo, Grammy Award–winning music producer

"This autobiography offers an incredible inside look into the music business and the unforgettable moments that shaped the sound of the '70s, '80s and beyond. Experience Ralph Johnson's story in his own words and enjoy!"

—Howard Hewett, singer-songwriter

"Never out of step, never out of time, never too much in a hurry. Ralph's rhythm and timing are next to perfection, honed in a band guided by spirituality that always made room for creativity and invention. Pure rhythm, pure fire in harmony."

—Reggie Calloway, singer-songwriter and producer

"Ralph Johnson is a hometown hero from Los Angeles and Inglewood, who helped shape the timeless sound of Earth, Wind & Fire—uplifting generations through music rooted in soul, unity, and joy."

—Representative Maxine Waters, 43rd Congressional District (CA), US House of Representatives

"Ralph Johnson is a wonderful musician and a wonderful personality. As he was part of one of the best bands ever, Earth, Wind & Fire, he's definitely of hero status!"

—Ray Parker Jr., musician and songwriter

"As a founder of one of the most iconic music groups in American history, Ralph Johnson offers the public an unflinching view into the tremendous highs and difficult lows of Earth, Wind & Fire. The reader will come away with a newfound respect of the personal toll and enormous work ethic required to become music legends."

—Roland Martin, political commentator and founder of Black Star Network

"I've had the pleasure of knowing, loving, and working with Ralph for more decades than I care to admit. He was then, and still is, the epitome of cool!"

—Siedah Garrett, singer and co-songwriter of "Man in the Mirror"

"Ralph Johnson is not only an important and longtime member of EWF, but he has kept his finger on the pulse of jazz as a drummer and his ear to the ground regarding the current, killin' musical talent that's out there! Ralph KNOWS."

—John Clayton, jazz musician, classical double bassist, arranger, and composer

"Ralph Johnson is one passionate individual, whether it be creating some of the greatest music ever recorded or as a practitioner and expert in martial arts. Did I mention his love for jazz? A true artist in more ways than one."

—Stephen "The Fight Professor" Quadros, drummer, actor, and combat sports broadcaster

RHYTHM & FIRE

A LIFE IN HARMONY WITH EARTH, WIND & FIRE

RALPH JOHNSON
WITH RORY PULLENS

FOREWORD BY QUESTLOVE

DIVERSION
BOOKS

Diversion Books
A division of Diversion Publishing Corp.
www.diversionbooks.com

For more information, email info@diversionbooks.com

First Diversion Books Edition: May 2026
Hardcover ISBN: 979-8-89515-143-3
e-ISBN: 979-8-89515-137-2

Design by Westchester Publishing Services
Cover design by Jonathan Sainsbury // 6x9 design
Cover design consultation with Ajay Peckham

Printed in the United States of America
1 3 5 7 9 10 8 6 4 2

Dedicated to my wife and sons:

Merced Suesannett Johnson
John-Ralph Johnson
Mark-Anthony Johnson

and my grandchildren:

Emuna Basya
Ariella Tzipora
Aaron David
Avraham Yehoshua
Askia Line
Adisa Cecil

Table of Contents

FOREWORD

By Questlove

Ralph Johnson's memoir is about elements. Elements in the astrological sense—earth, wind, and fire, the name of the band that brought him to prominence—but also the elements of the band's songs that drew me into their world. My musical memories start around age three. That's when I was at home with my parents starting to study album covers and song structures. Earth, Wind & Fire were a central part of my education, and there are specific moments in their music that hit me at a deeper level. They are, not surprising, drummer moments furnished by Ralph: the hi-hats in "Mighty Mighty," those eighth-note patterns, and the backward cymbals in the third verse of "Fair but So Uncool." The former was the very first drum pattern that I tried to figure out how to master when I was playing my pan-chair-furniture kit in my West Philadelphia household. The latter was surprising and strange to my ear, to the point I have always been obsessed with that sound. This is a very African origin story, drawn by the drums.

The book is also about spirit. Spirit in the religious sense, but also in the personal sense. Ralph Johnson embodies spirit and positivity. He is a student of the world who was, from a young age, perfectly poised to absorb experience and become a teacher, whether in the classroom or on the radio. I am especially moved by one moment in this memoir where he talks about the importance of connecting with others through music. "I want to be remembered as a man who didn't just perform, but *served*—someone always ready to jump in, to help, to offer something of value to those around me," he writes. "I've always been drawn to people, and I've always believed in showing up where I'm needed. Yes, I love music. But you know what I might love even more? Teaching music. Helping others. Passing it on. Unlocking it for someone else. Watching a student's eyes light up when they find their rhythm—when their hands hit the drums and something *clicks*. That, to me, is holy. That's true legacy."

The book is about harmony. Harmony in the musical sense, but also in the interpersonal sense. This is a story of collaborating with others, working toward a common goal in the most complex and beautiful ways possible. Harmony is sometimes invisible when it's there and most visible when it leaves. In the years following Maurice White's surprise dissolution of the band in the early eighties, Ralph had to reckon with disorientation and disappointment, to keep his life moving and his family supported without a clear sense of what will happen to the band—and the band of brothers—that he has been with for a decade. I won't ruin the suspense, but suffice it to say that Ralph has a way of finding his bearings.

Last, and by no means least, the book is about reflection. Reflection in the sense of introspection but also in the sense of mirrors. Ralph gives intimate and thoughtful details about every stage of his life, professional and personal. Near the end of the book, Ralph talks about the Earth, Wind & Fire documentary that I directed. The fact that he has nice things to say about it is great, but that's not the point. The point is how much Ralph's journey predicted and prepared my own. I think of all the moments in his life and career when he was forced to pivot. He joined a band with a strong front man who also happened to be a drummer. Later, when they broke up, he went out on his own as a producer and had success working with artists like the Temptations and Howard Hewett. The version of me that came to Ralph when I was making the documentary also benefitted from, and had to reflect on, these same shifts—there I was, a drummer-turned-filmmaker, or was that a filmmaker with a history of a drummer? I wasn't the first drummer asked to pivot to a role better suited to him. It reminds me of the first line of "Imagination," a song from the band's 1976 album *Spirit*: "Magic mirror, come and search my heart." Ralph searched his, and *Rhythm & Fire* is the result.

PROLOGUE

On a crisp December evening in 2019, as winter's chill whispered through the historic streets of Washington, DC, I found myself seated beneath the glowing chandeliers of the John F. Kennedy Center for the Performing Arts—a venue I had visited before, but never quite like this. That night, my heart swelled with a quiet, surreal pride as I sat with two of my original Earth, Wind & Fire bandmates—lead singer Philip Bailey and bassist Verdine White—to receive a level of recognition that, even after all we'd accomplished, still felt dreamlike.

We had come a long way from our early days, experimenting with rhythms, blending genres, building something timeless from scratch. Half a century had passed since we'd first taken the stage together, driven by little more than faith, sweat, and an uncompromising belief in the power of music to uplift. Now, fifty years later—with seven Grammy Awards behind us, over 100 million albums sold across the globe, multiple smash hits, ASCAP, NAACP, and BET honors, a Grammy Lifetime Achievement Award, an induction into the Rock & Roll Hall of Fame, a star embedded on the Hollywood Walk of Fame, and thousands of sold-out shows that spanned continents and generations—here we were, being honored at the Kennedy Center.

It wasn't just another accolade. It felt different. Deeper. The Kennedy Center Honors weren't about commercial success or radio spins. They were about artistic legacy—about the way music, film, and performance could shape culture, touch souls, and become part of the very DNA of a country. To be recognized on that stage, in that room, among those luminaries, was something I had never dared to imagine in the early days, when we were hauling gear in the back of vans, unsure if anyone would even show up.

The grandeur of the Concert Hall shimmered all around us—velvet seats filled with dignitaries, celebrities, fellow artists, and old friends. There was a subtle electricity in the air, not from nerves, but from reverence. The audience took their seats, dressed in tuxedos and evening gowns, faces lit with expectation. We weren't the only ones being celebrated that night. The spotlight would also shine on the indomitable actress Sally Field, the iconic voice of Linda Ronstadt, the revolutionary creators of the beloved children's series *Sesame Street*, and the visionary conductor-composer Michael Tilson Thomas.

It was a gathering of greatness—each honoree representing not just achievement, but endurance, evolution, and impact. And as I sat there in the Honorees' box, watching the lights dim and the opening notes of the tribute begin to rise, I couldn't help but feel that this was about reflection—on where we had come from, who we had become, and the music that had carried us all the way here.

I still couldn't believe it, wrapped in the glow of one of the most prestigious nights of my life, sitting there in that Honorees' box. It felt surreal. I've been on some legendary stages. I've stood before hundreds of thousands of people, traveled the world more times than I can count, shared grooves with the best musicians alive . . . but *this*? This was different. This wasn't just another performance or another accolade. This was the Kennedy Center Honors—the highest artistic recognition you can receive in the United States. In our world, it's the closest thing to being knighted. Everything else? Just another concert. This was a *cultural moment.*

Phil, Verdine, and I sat side by side, and it hit me—we were being celebrated not for a hit single or a chart position, but for the entire journey. For the work. For the soul we poured into it. For fifty years of music, sweat, creativity, love, and legacy. It was a moment not just for Earth, Wind & Fire, but for everyone who ever believed in us, danced with us, healed through our songs, or made babies to our ballads.

And then the show began. When sixteen-time Grammy winner David Foster opened the tribute by telling the story of how he pitched us "After the Love Has Gone"—in the late 1970s, a song that would go on to become his *first* Grammy-winning composition and one for us—I leaned back in my seat and smiled. I remembered that conversation. I remembered Maurice listening intently to Foster's pitch, always scanning for *feeling*. He knew a good song when he heard one—and that one hit us right in the heart. Hearing Foster recount that memory on this night, in that hall, with the entire world watching . . . That's when I knew: This night was going to live in me forever.

And while my body was in DC, wearing a tux, nodding politely in that dignified Honorees' box, my mind was scribbling memories in invisible ink. I couldn't stop the flood. I thought about all the people who helped shape me—not just musically, but fundamentally. And as always, my thoughts landed on the two most important people in my life—my parents.

That's where it all started. In the home. My childhood wasn't lavish, but it was rich—filled with discipline, music, laughter, and love. My parents were humble, hardworking, grounded people who believed in showing up—for work, for family, for life. They gave me structure. They gave me my first sense of rhythm—not on the drums, but in the daily beat of responsibility and pride. They weren't there physically that night, but believe me, they were *with* me. In that velvet-lined box seat, next to the weight of history, I could feel their presence so clearly it almost knocked the wind out of me.

Then came the first musical number. And who else but John Legend—one of the rare and brilliant EGOT (Emmy, Grammy, Oscar, Tony) winners—took the stage to perform "Can't Hide Love." Let me tell you, when John Legend sings your song, you *know* you've made it.

His version wasn't a copy. It was a reinterpretation—smooth, thoughtful, full of soul, just like him. It took me back. But not just to the studio in 1975. No—it took me *way* back. Suddenly, I was sitting in a tiny Los Angeles public school classroom in the sixth grade, listening to my teacher, Mrs. Johnson (no relation) guiding me through fractions and paragraphs I couldn't quite get a grip on. I had been struggling with reading and math, just enough that it started to wear on my confidence. But Mrs. Johnson saw something in me. She created what she called her "learning capsules," these little mini sessions she'd do with kids like me who just needed a bit more time, a little more care.

She helped me catch up. More than that—she helped me *believe* I could catch up.

And that belief followed me into every rehearsal, every studio session, every solo. Without my teacher, Mrs. Johnson, there might not have been a Ralph Johnson of Earth, Wind & Fire. I don't say that lightly. She showed me the power of education, of nurturing, of truly *seeing* someone. That's one of the reasons I've always had such a strong interest in teaching, mentoring, and helping others grow. Because someone once did that for me.

As the music swelled and John Legend hit those notes, I just kept thinking: *How did I get so lucky?* Why *me*? Why was I so fortunate to become part of one of the most magical, mystical, genre-bending, era-defining musical acts in history? I didn't have the full answer. But I knew it wasn't luck. It was people. It was purpose. It was timing. And maybe, just maybe, it was destiny.

Famed illusionist David Copperfield took the stage and shared how we were the first group to incorporate magic into our live performances. Magic, mystique, Egyptian culture, and mythology influenced our costumes and album covers. Was my musical destiny wrapped up in this magic?

Broadway Tony Award winner Cynthia Erivo sauntered onto the stage in a mesmerizing sequined silver-and-black outfit, singing our hit "Fantasy." Yet my life was no fantasy. It was one of purpose and design, shaped by a power higher and greater than any magic. Erivo transitioned into our smash hit "Reasons." I don't know the reason why I was selected into EWF in 1971, but I do know it wasn't magic; it wasn't luck.

The success of EWF was always the right combination of circumstances, events, and plans. I like to say we were the right group at the right time with the right sound at the right record company with the right president of that record company. It was divine fate. I believe there was no luck involved. My Vietnam experience taught me that. Yes, Vietnam. I believe that God always had his hand in my life, and it was He who brought me to Earth, Wind & Fire. After I graduated from high school in 1969, I was drafted into the military in 1971, receiving my 1-A draft notice. The war was still raging in 1971, and I was twenty years old. I came from a military family, so I knew it didn't get any worse than a 1-A notice. That simply meant that I was going to serve. There was no discussion, no alternative. Resigned to fulfill my duty to country, I had gone through the whole process of induction right down to going to the induction center on Wilshire Boulevard and completing my physical, which I passed with flying colors. I was on my way.

I was seriously thinking about going to a recruitment office—Air Force or Navy—to let them know that I'd rather not be drafted into the Army—not this way—so I would try and switch out and make a deal to join another branch. My older and younger brothers were both in the Air Force. I had no disdain for service. I had family members who served. Of course, I was hoping to launch further into my musical career, but that seemed like a fading thought at the time. Then, seemingly out of nowhere, I received a second letter that changed my classification to 1-H, which meant not subject to processing for induction.

I'm sitting at home thinking, "What happened? How could this be?" It appeared I was off the hook, for the time being anyway, but I didn't know why. The explanation was nothing short of a miracle. It turned out that during the period when I was drafted, there was supposed to be a ninety-day moratorium on getting drafted. There was supposed to be no drafting during this time, but the Selective Service kept the process going; they kept drafting. I found out later that six guys who were also being drafted, got wind of this and took the Selective Service to court, sued them, and won the case. Ten thousand of us got off and never had to serve. The next year, 1972, Richard Nixon was reelected president and ended the draft.

I have one of the greatest non-Vietnam stories ever told. I was claimed victor before I ever had to fight. I was delivered like the young man Daniel in the Bible from the lion's den of the draft. It wasn't anything I did. It was God. He had a different plan for me, and He proved it. After that experience, I auditioned for Earth, Wind & Fire in that same year, 1971, and as they say, the rest is history.

If I had been drafted, I probably would have been in the military as a lifer. I would have done my twenty years and then come out to figure out the rest of my life. Or I would have been a professional chef, gone to culinary school, and done that, even internationally.

My wife says I would have made a great engineer, the way I think. I like to tinker; it's fun. I remember how my dad always built stuff around the house. It was hard for him to throw things away. There'd be old lumber, and he'd say he would use it later. Years would pass, and it would still be sitting there. No, I wouldn't become an engineer.

While these were all noble careers, my life was meant to take the direction it did, and I thank God for it. It was meant for me to make a positive difference on the global musical stage. I was supposed to be in Earth, Wind & Fire.

My mind jolted back to the present when R&B artist and three-time Grammy Award winner Ne-Yo took the stage and belted out our breakthrough No. 1 hit, "Shining Star." One by one, the usually reserved and stiff Kennedy Center audience began to get up from their seats and clap to the beat.

Ne-Yo next slid into our infectious hit "Sing a Song," bringing everyone to their feet. The audience loved it!

The Jonas Brothers stepped out and kept the party going with their rendition of our blockbuster hit, "Boogie Wonderland," a song we performed with The Emotions. Are those the Jonas Brothers singing an Earth, Wind & Fire song? It was another confirmation that our music was not just Black music; it was universal music, and our songs appealed to everyone. I felt the Jonas Brothers' closeness singing together as if they were the blood brothers they were. After five decades together, I was sitting with my brothers too, Phil and Verdine, representing our Earth, Wind & Fire band brothers who had changed the musical world.

In this instance, watching the Jonas Brothers perform, I recognized my accomplishment and felt good inside. If I could be remembered as an upstanding family man, a caring father, and a loving husband, then my family would have a proud legacy; my parents would be proud, and all who mattered to me would feel in some satisfying way what I was feeling now.

Our music was just as relevant that night as it was the day those songs first hit the airwaves. I felt it in the way the audience responded. It wasn't just nostalgia. It wasn't just a celebration of a bygone era. The music still *lived*. It *breathed*. It danced through the room and into people's hearts like it always had.

I've always believed that the true magic of Earth, Wind & Fire was not just about sound—it was about *feeling*. People don't just listen to our music. They *invite* it into their lives. They dance to it at weddings. They play it at family reunions, at backyard cookouts, during moments of joy and celebration—and sometimes even during the hard times, when a good groove can remind you that you're still here, still moving. From the very beginning, our music gave off what I like to call "feel-good energy." That wasn't an accident. And somehow, after all these decades, it still works. It still lifts spirits.

That night, you could see it on people's faces—in the way they clapped, swayed, sang along. The connection was still alive, still electric. That's not something you can fake. And that's when I felt something else, too—something bittersweet but beautiful.

I couldn't take credit for this moment—not without first honoring the man who made it all possible—Maurice White. He was the nucleus. The architect. The dreamer with the blueprint no one else could see until he built it around us. Maurice had *the vision*—and it wasn't just musical. It was *spiritual*. He believed in sound as a form of healing, rhythm as a universal language, and harmony as a kind of medicine. He didn't just put a band together—he put together a *movement*. He assembled personalities, cultures, philosophies, and frequencies, and somehow made it all make sense.

I missed him so much that night. God, I wanted him there—physically, tangibly, sitting next to us, nodding with that calm, knowing smile of his. But then I realized . . . he *was* there.

His spirit filled that hall. You could *feel* him in the air. I saw his smile reflected in the faces of strangers. I heard his laughter tucked into the horns, his soul in every lyric. That night wasn't just a tribute to us—it was a homecoming for him. And there was no question in my mind that this was Maurice's night, too.

And yet, in the midst of all this glory and celebration, I found myself wondering—*quietly*—what about me? Not in an ego way, but in a legacy way.

What would I leave behind?

Earth, Wind & Fire will be remembered—no doubt about that. Our music has already outlived so many eras, and it'll keep playing long after we're gone. But what about Ralph Johnson—the man behind the drums, the vocalist up front, the songwriter/producer?

What will they say about me? I hope they say I was intelligent. Not just book-smart, but wise in the ways that matter. I hope they say I was articulate—able to speak thoughtfully, with care and curiosity. I'd love for them to say I had a sense of humor—that I didn't take myself *too* seriously, that I could find joy even when things were heavy.

But beyond all that, I hope they remember me as someone creative. Someone who always brought something new to the table. Someone who cared deeply—about the music, about the people, about the message.

I want to be remembered as a man who didn't just perform, but *served*—someone always ready to jump in, to help, to offer something of value to those around me. I've always been drawn to people, and I've always believed in showing up where I'm needed. Yes, I love music. But you know what I might love even more? Teaching music. Helping others. Passing it on. Unlocking it for someone else. Watching a student's eyes light up when they find their rhythm—when their hands hit the drums and something *clicks*. That, to me, is holy. That's true legacy.

If someone out there, years from now, says, "Ralph Johnson helped me find my voice through music," well . . . I think I'd be okay with that.

I think I'd be more than okay. Because in the end, life isn't just about the notes you play—it's about the lives you touch in between the beats.

I gingerly glanced to my side to see where my wife, Susie, was standing in celebration with us. My life's most cherished accomplishment was keeping my family intact through the good and bad, joyous times and challenging ones, and being married to my wife for forty years. I was able to raise my sons, and they turned out to be outstanding individuals. I was blessed to be able to give them everything they needed to keep moving forward. That's a life achievement. That's something to celebrate. Holding the family bond together requires commitment. I couldn't help but dwell on my wife's commitment over the decades. Susie sacrificed so much for me and my musical dreams. One of her biggest sacrifices was giving up companionship because I was gone on tour so often. Maybe from a material standpoint, she didn't suffer because she had everything she needed to take care of the boys, but I missed graduations, birthdays, and family get-togethers.

That had greater value than money. I know Susie explained it to them, yet I hated to be gone for those things. But I had to do what I had to do. That was my sacrifice. We believed that the boys understood because they saw me at work when Susie would take them to concerts. Still, it was a major sacrifice. Anyone can bring babies into the world, but can everyone raise them and affect their thinking positively, exposing them to the things that matter so that when they go out into the world, they do great things and contribute to society on a positive level?

Host of the evening, LL Cool J, a Kennedy Center honoree himself, returned to the stage with the full array of performers joining him for the event-ending finale, our concert signature song, "September." The audience erupted into a joyful celebration. Everyone, including us, was on their feet. Earth, Wind & Fire, as a group, and as individuals, were in the September of our lives, but we weren't done yet. The performers onstage were in unison echoing lyric lines, "Do you remember . . . 21st night of September? / Love was changing the mind of pretenders / While chasing the clouds away / Our hearts were ringing / In the key that our souls were singing / As we danced in the night / Remember, how the stars stole the night away, yeah, yeah, yeah / Hey, hey, hey / Ba-dee-ya, say, do you remember? / Ba-dee-ya, dancin' in September / Ba-dee-ya, never was a cloudy day." I do remember so many things—the ceremony of having our portrait inducted into the Smithsonian Portrait Gallery in Washington, DC, to be preserved forever in their permanent collection. I do remember receiving my honorary doctorate from Columbia College in Chicago for my exemplary musicianship as part of a group that changed how music was presented on record and in live performance, and for now, being able to do it for fifty-plus years.

As each artist basked in their due spotlight, the energy in the room rose higher and higher. We were the final performers to be honored, and the room, filled with celebrities, policymakers, and prominent philanthropists, was ready to erupt into a full-blown party. Although that night captured our group's musical achievements, as well as the hearts of everyone there, my mind drifted to what our revered leader and group founder, Maurice White, who had passed away three years earlier, had instilled in me as a mentor and guide some fifty years ago. My thoughts reached far beyond this captivating evening party scene and the musical group that had brought me fame and fortune. During these moments, several questions raced through my mind: How did this everyday Los Angeleno get here? Who and what shaped my life perspectives to help me reach this point? Was I just one of the lucky ones, or did I owe my success to something greater? What was my purpose now that I "made it"? Was tonight about me or about others I inspired? Was Earth, Wind & Fire the culmination of my legacy, or did I have another chapter to open?

After that night, I knew it was time to share the story of Ralph Johnson—original member, drummer, percussionist, singer, and songwriter of the mega group Earth,

Wind & Fire. This story is also about my life beyond music, too—my lifelong love of learning, teaching, travel, art collecting, scuba diving, martial arts, and money management—and I hope it will provide insights that will promote growth.

Part One

EARTH

Chapter 1

Shining Star

We musicians know the stage has always had its own weather. I'm often asked what it's like to play our hit "Shining Star" live. I always smile first. Before I can form the words, the memories come in waves—lights, heat, vibration, and that unmistakable punch of Al McKay's opening guitar riff cutting through the air like a flare shot into a dark sky. But to truly explain what it *feels* like, I have to go back into the body—the heartbeat, the rhythm, the sweat that gathers between your shoulders just before a show, the sense that something electric is building in the space between you and tens of thousands of expectant faces.

Even after decades onstage, the moment right before the downbeat of "Shining Star" has a very particular weight to it. Maurice, Larry Dunn, and Philip wrote this tune like you're greeting an old friend who's walked beside you for most of your life. It's a song with muscle, with stride, with its own confident grin. And when we were out there onstage—Maurice, Verdine, Philip, the horns, the whole universe of Earth, Wind & Fire on one stage—there was nothing like it.

You could feel the heat radiating up from the lights as if the floor itself were warming beneath your feet. A murmur filled the arena—a mixture of conversations, laughter, footsteps, the clatter of last-minute adjustments from the crew. Sometimes I'd look out before the house lights dropped and catch sight of a little kid perched on a parent's shoulders, wearing a T-shirt three sizes too big, eyes bright. That always grounded me. It reminded me that this music wasn't just a performance; it was a bridge across generations.

Backstage, I went through the same ritual every night. A few stretches. A shakeout of the wrists. Close my eyes. Breathe in the pulse of the crowd. Drummers carry time, and I've always believed that means we carry responsibility too. We anchor everything. The horns, the vocals, Verdine's bass—every piece relies on the pocket being tight enough to build on. And "Shining Star"? That pocket is pure joy, pure drive. So I centered myself.

And then the lights went out.

A wave of sound hit like a living thing—cheers, screams, applause rising in a single upward sweep. It never gets old. That's the truth. You could be tired, jet-lagged, hungry for sleep, and the moment those lights dropped, all of that slipped away. The music took over.

The guitar riff started first—bright, sharp, funky. Even after hearing it thousands of times, it still had a way of jolting the air awake. Verdine usually stepped forward the moment it hit, dancing like the groove was lifting him right off the stage. The crowd recognized the song instantly. You'd see the wave travel outward—hands in the air, people bouncing to their feet, heads turning toward each other as if to say, *"Here it comes."* That's the moment you know the song belongs to them as much as it does to you.

My entrance came with the drums—tight, punchy, forward-driving. When I brought the beat in, it felt like opening a door and letting energy flood through. The kick drum thumped against my chest with each pulse. The snare cracked sharp as a whip. The hi-hat sizzled like it had its own current running through it. Every part of the kit vibrated in harmony with the band, with the stage, with the audience.

I could always feel Maurice's presence before I saw him—he had that gravitational pull. When he stepped to the mic and belted the first lines, the audience erupted again, louder, fuller. His voice—strong, warm, unmistakably Maurice—rode over the groove like it had been forged for that very moment. There's a moment during every live performance when the barrier between stage and audience disappears. With "Shining Star," that moment arrived fast—sometimes within seconds. You'd look out and feel the entire crowd move in a single rhythm. Thousands of faces lit by stage reflections, thousands of shoulders swaying, thousands of voices singing the lines right back at us. There's nothing quite like that. It's like steering a ship powered by collective joy.

I felt their energy physically. When I hit the floor toms, the vibrations bounced back at me from the audience. When the crowd jumped, I felt the stage tremble beneath my feet. Their voices didn't just rise—they wrapped around us, filling the air pockets between every note we played.

And I played harder. Not out of effort, but because the energy demanded it. "Shining Star" is a celebration; it lifts people. The funk, the forward drive, the optimism—it all becomes a single force pushing outward. There's a kind of meditation in drumming. People think it's all adrenaline, but inside the music there's a deep, still center. While my arms were moving, my feet pumping the kick pedal, my body locking into the groove, another part of me floated above the whole scene, noticing everything.

I'd see Verdine spin sideways, his bass practically glowing under the lights. I'd catch Philip raising his arm to signal the horn section, that little flick he always had. And the horns—my God, the horns—would come in like a gleaming burst of color, slicing through the air with precision.

I kept the beat steady beneath it all. Even when the tempo pushed with excitement or the crowd surged louder, my job was to keep the foundation strong. But I didn't just keep time—I *felt* time. I shaped it. Each note was a conversation, not just with the band but with the past, with every audience we'd played for, with the first moment that riff was ever recorded.

There were nights when the groove felt so good that we all exchanged glances onstage—those silent, knowing looks. *Tonight's one of those nights.* And when that happened, the song felt almost . . . alive. I always knew when "Shining Star" reached its breaking point—the moment where the energy didn't just rise but *lifted.* That was usually around the chorus, when the vocals, the horns, the guitars, the bass, the keys, and the percussion all braided together into a single unstoppable force. When we'd hit the line "You're a shining star, no matter who you are," something always happened in the air. It felt like the room inhaled deeply as one, like those words resonated far beyond the melody. That lyric, that message—it's the reason the song keeps living. It lifts people because it tells them *they* matter, *they* shine, *they* are part of something bigger.

"Shining Star" is tight, structured funk, but live performance always gives room for freedom. Sometimes the guitar would stretch a phrase, teasing the crowd. Sometimes Verdine would add a flourish that made the bassline dance a little wilder. Sometimes Philip or Maurice would let the audience take over entire lines.

And as they did, I adjusted. Drumming live is a conversation. The band speaks, the crowd responds, and I keep the language flowing. Increase the kick to match the energy. Pull the snare back a fraction to let a vocal run breathe. Open the hi-hat just slightly to make the groove shimmer. These minor choices were invisible to most but deeply felt in the body of the music.

Those little musical choices—that's where the magic lived. By the time we approached the final chorus, the entire room usually felt like a furnace of light and movement. Sweat rolled down my arms. The sticks felt warm and familiar in my hands, worn smooth from years of playing. My shoulders worked in steady motion, precise yet fluid.

Onstage, everything tightened for the last push. The horns punched brighter. The vocals rose higher. The bass locked in with me, Verdine's energy still somehow escalating even after a full show. And I drove the rhythm like a heartbeat accelerating at just the right moment.

In those final repetitions—"Shining star for you to see . . ."—I'd look across the stage and catch Maurice smiling. That smile said everything: *We're here. We're doing what we love. And look at what we've created.*

Then we'd hit the last hits together—clean, powerful, unified. The final crash of the cymbal would ring out into the arena like a flare dissolving in the night sky.

When the last note faded, the audience roared. That sound—waves of applause crashing forward—was something I felt deep inside. The lights would shift, bathing the stage in warm gold. My pulse slowed from a sprint to a steady jog. I'd wipe my brow, take a breath, and smile. Because in that moment, I always felt connected to something larger than myself. "Shining Star" isn't just a song—it's an affirmation, a reminder, a celebration. And every time we performed it, I felt privileged to be part of the force that carried it into people's lives.

People often imagine that the best part of performing is the applause. Don't get me wrong—the applause is beautiful. But the true magic lies in the moments *during* the music, when everything aligns: the musicianship, the energy, the message, the collective heartbeat of the audience. That's the place where ego fades and the music speaks. Playing "Shining Star" live was stepping into that place every night. I feel the message of the song—its optimism, its brightness—radiating outward. That message wasn't just sung. It was lived.

It was shared. And for those few minutes onstage, we were all shining stars.

Despite the stage lights, the live audience, and the sweat rolling off my face, I felt at home on the drum throne that night, almost like I was back at my childhood home on Hobart Boulevard in Los Angeles, practicing with my first snare and chasing my childhood dream.

Chapter 2

Hobart Boulevard

Ralph's a fantastic person, very smart, intelligent, and articulate. He's a master of many things. He's a lovable person as a brother, but I thank God for his kindness and generosity to his fans. He's a celebrity, but a real person first.

—Pam Johnson, sister

My story begins on Hobart Boulevard, long before the lights, long before the drum risers, long before the magic of Earth, Wind & Fire swept me into its orbit. If I close my eyes, I can still smell the sweetness of the loquat tree in our backyard—the kind of sweetness that lingers on your fingers even after you're done picking fruit. Our neighbors had a fig tree whose branches leaned over the fence as if trying to join our family. And honestly, that was the vibe of our block: homes leaning into each other, kids drifting in and out of porches, life unfolding at an easy, generous pace.

My parents—Jesse and Grace Johnson—were two Southern souls who carried the quiet dignity of people who had seen hard things but chose joy anyway. My father, a tough ex–Army sergeant from Georgia, had fought in the South Pacific during World War II. But at home, he carried a softness in his hands, a patience in his smile. My mother, Grace, came from Mound Bayou, Mississippi, with a voice that could warm a sanctuary and a backbone made of pure conviction. They met after the war, fell in love, and, for reasons they never fully explained, moved out to Los Angeles—maybe for opportunity, maybe for freedom, maybe simply to build a life without small-town eyes watching every move they made.

Whatever the reason, LA became the place where they planted their roots. My mom sorted mail at the post office before she retired into motherhood. My father worked long hours as a chair car porter on the Southern Pacific railroad. When those Sunset Limited and Golden State Limited trains rolled into Union Station, my brother and I would stand waiting, watching the passengers spill out, each of them stepping into their next chapter while my father stepped back into ours.

Some of my favorite childhood memories are tied to those trains. I remember the rumble under my feet, the smell of iron and oil, the way travelers looked like characters in stories I was too young to understand. There was that one trip to Sacramento, the state capital, where we received certificates with our names written in calligraphy that made me feel like royalty. I took mine to school for Show-and-Tell, and the other kids stared wide-eyed. No one else I knew had been to Sacramento.

But I had.

My parents didn't have fancy titles or high-paying jobs, but what they *did* have was each other—and they knew how to make a simple life feel full. My mom made fig preserves with the fruit from our neighbor's tree. My father would gather ingredients for her holiday fruitcakes and brew strong eggnog for New Year's, pairing it with pigs' feet simmered until the whole house smelled like tradition. He'd take me fishing and come home with bags full of barracuda, sheepshead, mackerel—fish that looked like they belonged in a tall tale.

They weren't wealthy, but they were rich. And they were rich in all the ways that matter.

They stayed together into their nineties, working, loving, living, and teaching—never by lecture but by example. Their message, which I absorbed without even knowing it, was simple: Work hard. Work honestly. And you can turn effort into opportunity.

We stayed on Hobart Boulevard until 1966, but 1961 is the year that glows brightest in my memory. I was eight years old and woke up before dawn on Christmas morning, carried by that electric hope only kids know. And there, under the tree, waiting like destiny itself, was a snare drum from a company called Regency. It wasn't one of the top brands, but it was mine.

I didn't know it yet, but my parents saw something in me—the rhythm always tapping through my fingers, the beats I'd build on the kitchen table, the patterns I'd drum into my schoolbooks. And when they took me downtown to the Southern California Music Company, I was mesmerized. The brass instruments smelled like lacquer and possibility. I didn't understand it then, but that place stirred something in me deeper than fascination. It stirred purpose.

The next Christmas, the snare became a full St. George drum set. Lessons followed. Practice became my favorite form of play. And before long, at my constant urgings, my father traded that St. George set for a Ludwig kit—my first true musical love.

One of the first beats I learned was a bossa nova from Cannonball Adderley's "Jive Samba." Truth be told, it probably sounded like thunder rolling down a staircase, but my parents never told me to quiet down.

"Play, Ralph," my mother would say. "Play." To her, noise was music waiting for its shape.

My sister Pam remembers watching me spin records like a DJ, practice until my arms were tired, lose myself in rhythm. Years later, she told me: "I always knew you were going to be something. I just didn't know what." She listed everything she thought made me unique—my cooking, my fast driving, my chess boards, my art collections, my martial arts, my scuba diving. But through all of that, the drums always had my heart.

By fourth grade, I knew exactly who I was going to be. Not hoped—knew. My childhood friend Sharon remembered a moment when she found me playing piano while other kids made popcorn balls and Kool-Aid concoctions. I turned to her and said, calm as a preacher delivering a truth: "I'm going to be a famous musician." It wasn't arrogance. It wasn't fantasy. It was the soul recognizing itself.

I kept studying drummers—Tony Williams, Roy Haynes, Jack DeJohnette, Buddy Rich. I'd sit with their records trying to decode every sticking pattern. Philly Joe Jones became a kind of musical puzzle for me; I'd listen over and over, trying to understand how he did what he did.

But the moment that changed the trajectory of my young life came on January 1, 1966, when my friend Arthur Copper and I went to a James Brown concert. That night, for the first time, I saw three drum sets on one stage. Three. James Brown didn't just have a band. He had an army. I remember staring at that ticket—JAMES BROWN—and thinking, "*Maybe one day someone will hold a ticket with my name on it.*"

Meanwhile, music was everywhere in our home. My older brother Ronald, a USC graduate, Air Force cadet, and later a lieutenant in the LAPD, brought home jazz albums—Miles Davis, Coltrane, the Modern Jazz Quartet. My father loved big band swing and once brought home Benny Goodman's *Live at the Brussels World's Fair 1958.* That album—especially "Sing, Sing, Sing," with Roy Burns on drums—became my personal master class.

Back in those days, I was also listening to Philly Joe Jones. I was listening to him solo. I thought he was very interesting. Sometimes, a drummer will play some stuff, and you'll hear them do stuff in a solo and you can't necessarily decode it. I wanted to figure out what they did and what the sticking was. Was it two rights on the left or was it right, left, left, left, right? What was it? You know, so in listening to Philly Joe Jones, I felt like I had a chance at decoding what he was doing. I'd go buy a record, sit down with it, and try to emulate what I was hearing.

For me, he was the most accessible out of all the drummers I listed. Second, I would go with probably Elvin Jones, who played with John Coltrane. It was Elvin Jones on drums, Jimmy Garrison on bass, McCoy Tyner on piano, and the great John Coltrane on tenor saxophone. And so that, the Elvin Jones stuff I like, too. It was Elvin and Philly, if I just had to narrow it down.

Jack DeJohnette was also a favorite of mine, and I learned so much from him. He wound up playing with the great Keith Jarrett, the Keith Jarrett Trio, and I love Keith Jarrett as a pianist. That was quite a trio. My favorite configuration is a trio, and I always wanted to play with Keith Jarrett. It doesn't look like I'm going to be able to do that because Keith has had a couple of strokes. He doesn't even play anymore. But man, if I could just play with Keith Jarrett. I really admired Jack DeJohnette because he was his drummer. With that trio—Keith Jarrett on piano, Gary Peacock on bass, Jack DeJohnette on drums—you have some wonderful things going on.

Years later, I met Roy Burns at NAMM and told him he was one of the reasons I played drums. It was emotional—one of those rare moments when you get to thank the person whose sound shaped your destiny.

My childhood wasn't just music. I played baseball—third base and pitcher for a Little League team called the Christians, a name none of us kids thought was cool. I was a Boy Scout, learned my knots, learned to swim at the 28th Street

YMCA. But no matter what else I did, the drumbeat always pulled me back.

In 1966, my parents moved us to Inglewood, to Ninetieth Street and Eighth Avenue. That move changed everything. I started at Morningside High School, and I often joke that those years felt like life without fences—both literally and spiritually. The world was shifting: Woodstock, Vietnam, Watts, the counterculture revolution. But inside that tumult, my music was blooming.

And years later, after my marching band experience, I was standing onstage with Earth, Wind & Fire, selling out the Forum for five nights. I found it hard to believe that we could do that, but we did. We were really, really pumped up about that. It was quite an accomplishment for us at that time. We pretty much were on top of the world, having sold out the Forum for five nights. The only other act that had done that was the Jacksons. There weren't many Black acts that could do that at the time in the late '70s. I couldn't help thinking back to those years when I watched the building rise from dirt and steel. Back when I didn't even know my life would one day lead me onto its stage.

I still remember the night my wife Susie took our oldest son John-Ralph to his first Earth, Wind & Fire show. Planets hanging in the air, band members descending from the heavens, the whole spectacular vision of our mystical era. My son's eyes were wide with wonder—until sleep claimed him halfway through. It was well past his bedtime, after all.

My success didn't arrive overnight. I stayed hungry. Focused. In love with the craft. Perhaps one of the secrets to my success was emulating my parents' work ethic. They taught me that it doesn't matter if your dreams are realized. What's important is that you make something of what you have at the moment. It's about being resourceful, creative, and persistent. It's about never giving up, even when the odds are against you. It's about acting, working hard, and maximizing what you have right now. If you do that, you can achieve anything you want.

I joined The Teen Turbans in 1966. We won a KHJ Radio Battle of the Bands—first place. We came in with showmanship; we were dressed, we did a whole thing, the whole presentation. We even got brand-new instruments for the competition. When word got out about the only Black band winning the competition, my popularity went through the roof. We didn't expect to win, but we did! Then came gigs across LA, nights at UCLA frat houses, late-night hangs at Tommy's Hamburgers and Johnny's Pastrami.

After that came The Mob, then The Master's Children, who took me to Las Vegas and, later, to Tokyo in 1969 and 1970—straight out of high school.

When I met drummer Louie Bellson of the Duke Ellington Orchestra, who was married to Pearl Bailey, the Master's Children came in to do a gig at the International Hotel in Las Vegas. Pearl was performing, and I remember going to her dressing room. I remember her saying, "All the stars are in the sky." I never forgot that. And I also never forgot that after my drum solo during our set, she pulled me to the side, and thinking I was going to get a compliment from the great Pearl Bailey, she politely said, "You should probably drop that solo because you're already onstage with one of the greatest drummers. You should let Louie have it."

"Okay, cool," I replied. "You got it." I didn't have enough ego to come back at Pearl. But inside, I knew what I could do. I understood. And I kept playing.

There was the time I was called last-minute to a television special at Caesars Palace. "Can you get to Vegas right now?" "Sure." "Can you read music?" "Yes, sir." I walked in, orchestra already seated, and I sat down behind the drums like I had been born there. "Count it off," I said. Confidence, not ego. I was prepared. And that's the thing—preparation.

My teacher, Clarence Johnston, drilled everything into me—technique, theory, showmanship. He taught greats. My classmates were Raymond Pounds, who would go on to play with Stevie Wonder, and Clayton Cameron, who would play with Sammy Davis Jr. and Tony Bennett. Johnston taught me. So when the moment came, I wasn't afraid to step into it.

Looking back on it all, my life reads like the lyrics to the song that would later define so much of what I believed: "You're a shining star / No matter who you are / Shining bright to see / What you could truly be / Shining star for you to see / What your life can truly be / Shining star for you to see / What your life can truly be."

I was that kid on Hobart Boulevard with a drum, a dream, and parents who believed in me before I even knew what believing meant. And they were right. I just kept playing.

The world was wide open and changing, and my attitude reflected this cultural change. This included my musical development. It, too, was wide open. No fences.

Chapter 3

The Grand Experiments

Ralph is present with everyone he interacts with. He connects with the human spirit of everyone he comes across. He's a great songwriter, lyricist, and a phenomenal teacher. He is the type of person that everyone will be a better human being for knowing him.

—Kenny Dickerson, photographer and drummer

After I graduated from high school in 1969, I continued to play with a band at Maverick's Flat in South LA, the West Coast version of New York's Apollo Theater. Back in the day, it's where Ike and Tina Turner would come and get in the groove. Muhammad Ali, between fights, would work as a disc jockey, doing his rhymes. The Rolling Stones, the Mamas and the Papas, Billy Preston, Rufus, the Whispers, Fifth Dimension, the Commodores, and even Parliament-Funkadelic tested out their high-energy stage shows there.

It was a venue of grand experiments, and it was usually so crowded that I couldn't know who was out there, if people were enjoying the energetic yet laid-back vibes, or if someone, by chance, might be checking me out. All I knew was that I was ready to play with some act as a professional drummer. I wanted to play pop/R&B, and I wanted to make a living as a musician.

After performing at Maverick's Flat for two years, I auditioned for Earth, Wind & Fire in 1971, and for over fifty years I've been making music for a living with one of the world's most popular, most recognized, and most innovative R&B groups in history.

Maurice White founded Earth, Wind & Fire in 1969. His passion for music grew during his high school days in Memphis, Tennessee. After high school, he moved to Chicago to study music at the Chicago Conservatory of Music, where he honed his drumming skills. In 1962, White joined a jazz trio, the Jazzmen, which later became the Pharaohs. Soon after he started playing as a studio musician at the legendary Chess Records, playing drums on the records of everyone from Etta James and Muddy Waters to the Impressions, Rotary Connection, and Betty Everett.

And then in 1966 Maurice joined Ramsey Lewis and his trio, won a Grammy with Ramsey, and discovered the kalimba, the African thumb piano that would become a signature sound for Earth, Wind & Fire. Maurice left Ramsey in 1969, moved to Los Angeles, and formed his own group, The Salty Peppers, with Wade Flemons and Don Whitehead. He soon changed the band's name to Earth, Wind & Fire after the three elements in his astrological chart. The new name also reflected Maurice's spiritual approach to music that would transcend all genres.

Maurice White had dismantled Earth, Wind & Fire in 1971 after the group recorded two albums with Warner Bros. Records. They knew they needed a drummer. As they started asking around, everyone said, "You gotta go check out Ralph Johnson." My audition for the group came at Michael Beal's home in Baldwin Hills. The audition consisted of Verdine White, the extraordinary bassist who was Maurice's brother, and the guitar player at that time, Michael Beal. The three of us jammed together. When it was over, Verdine called Maurice, and Maurice asked him what he thought.

"He's the cat," Verdine replied.

That was all that had to be said. Maurice responded, "Let's go with him then."

They asked me if I'd like to be a part of a new group. There was nothing left for me to say but "yes." What was I going to do? Sit around and play at a local club night after night? Yeah, right. It only made sense. I went forward as a musician, took the offer, and was going to see what happened.

In about a week, I packed up my drum set and just went from there. We started rehearsing. You know, we're all trying to figure it out. Maurice directed the rehearsal traffic. If the song we were working on didn't feel right, he would make some changes. He might come to me and correct a drum thing or go to a guitar player and correct something. That's how it went, but not in a dictatorial way. We were feeling each other out, hearing each other, and listening to one another, so when Michael took off on a riff, everyone knew where to fill in. We hadn't even gone to the studio yet because we were in between the Warner Bros. deal and the upcoming CBS deal where Clive Davis was still trying to work a contract out for us. We were rehearsing at this place called Moro Landis Dance Studio in Studio City. It took like six to eight months before we got in the studio. When we did get there though, I knew what I had. Apparently, it worked. I'm still here. I think it's actually very cool to say that, and it's the truth. I wasn't nervous. Not nervous at all. I was like, count it off, let's go. I like that, I like that. Really, I felt great.

As a band, you can rehearse, and rehearse, and rehearse, but there's a certain chemistry you're waiting to kick in. For us, it just hadn't kicked in yet. We were just too new. We were playing like a bunch of guys from over here and over there, just hoping, that at the end of the day, we were going to have something that would be remembered as memorable.

The first time we did a gig together was up in Oakland, at the Oakland Auditorium, I think it was called. We appeared there with this new band—which was nowhere near the band, what we call "the nine"—but we got booed. The crowd was chanting, "Bring back The Sisters Love," which was the act that went on before us. Man, that was so traumatic for our guitarist Michael Beal that he quit the band after that gig. That's when Roland Bautista joined us.

A funny story about that gig, too. There was no dressing room, so we were in the bathroom getting ready. A guy walks into the men's stall, but he's carrying a hi-hat cymbal. I'm, like, that's interesting; why is this guy walking into the stall with a hi-hat? Well, we go out onstage and my hi-hat has been stolen! It was my hi-hat the guy was carrying!

Maurice and Verdine were visionaries—always were. When Earth, Wind & Fire went through its early transformation, they didn't just want to rebuild the band. They wanted to elevate it. Reinvent it. They were thinking bigger than anyone else around us, and that kind of ambition takes courage. So when they headed out to Denver and met up with this smooth-voiced singer named Philip Bailey, things started to shift.

Philip was something else. He had this *otherworldly* falsetto, pure and piercing, but there was weight behind it too—like someone had wrapped gospel, jazz, and celestial energy into one voice. And he wasn't just a vocalist; he was a thinker, a spiritual guy. His presence alone changed the chemistry.

Now, what a lot of people don't realize is that Philip didn't come alone. He brought with him a young, ridiculously gifted pianist named Larry Dunn. Larry was this quiet genius—fingers like lightning, but always serving the groove, the melody, the mood. He could hear things the rest of us hadn't even imagined yet. And then Larry introduced us to Andrew Woolfolk—a saxophonist whose sound could slice through the sky. Andrew was cool, stylish, always on his own wavelength, and man, when he played, you *felt* it.

Maurice, being Maurice, wasn't just gathering talent—he was assembling a musical universe. So he reached back to his Chicago roots and pulled in some of his guys: Louis Satterfield, a beast on trombone, and the rest of the horn section that would soon become The Phenix Horns. That right there? That changed *everything.* Those horns didn't just accent the music—they *spoke.* They were like a voice of their own, a character in every song.

So now, we had this electrified lineup: young, raw, hungry, and *crazy* talented. Everybody brought something unique—a different rhythm, a different background, a different voice. The energy in rehearsals was explosive. Ideas bounced around like pinballs. Maurice kept the vision tight—disciplined—but he let us bring our full selves to the table.

We made an album. Then hit the road. Then another album. Then the road again. And suddenly, we weren't just a band anymore. We were a force.

The audiences got bigger, louder, more diverse. The music traveled across borders before we even got there. That mix of soul, funk, jazz, African rhythms, spirituality, style, power—no one else was doing it like that. And the chemistry? It was real. We weren't manufactured.

Those additions—Philip, Larry, Andrew, Al, Johnny, Fred, the Phenix Horns—they weren't just names on a roster. They were the *soul infusion* that helped Earth, Wind & Fire evolve into something global, spiritual, unstoppable. That lineup would go on to define our legacy.

Looking back, I realize that moment—that merging of vision and new blood—was the beginning of Earth, Wind & Fire as the world knows it today. It wasn't just about getting back on the road. It was about becoming a phenomenon.

Activity was happening on the studio front, too, because Maurice wanted to have various artists and musical groups making their albums in the same spaces. There was a lot of cross-fertilization back then, when we'd be hearing songs by the Emotions or Deniece Williams, and they'd be hearing us. As our studio manager Richie Salvato told me, "Back in those days, Complex Production Studios and Kalimba Productions, where Maurice worked, were in the same building. Whenever Maurice produced an album, it was under the Kalimba umbrella. Even Earth, Wind & Fire albums carried the logo 'produced by Maurice White for Kalimba Productions.' Maurice wanted to replicate a lot of what he had done growing up at Chess and Stax Records. He went to Bob Cavallo and said, 'I want to have a series of writing rooms and studios so we can create the music and then move down to the studios,' just like when he was a session drummer." Bob and Maurice wanted to take advantage of anything that would help them stay ahead in business. They would create in-house components that no other act had—their own booking agency that would book the tours, their own production company that would handle sound and lights.

Cavallo was a good friend of Walter Yetnikoff, the president of CBS/Columbia Records. Cavallo pitched that since Earth, Wind & Fire was one of the biggest acts on the planet, CBS should support them with a state-of-the-art studio, The Complex. In Richie Salvato's words: The Complex "had history right there in Beverly Hills on Charleville Blvd, the same building that Neil Bogart had for his label, Casablanca. The Complex would go on to experience everything—breakthroughs, late nights, laughter, arguments, triumphs. It was where the sound of Earth, Wind & Fire was shaped and refined. But they just didn't get a building. Yetnikoff threw in a record label they had in their vaults, ARC, to record artists. Earth, Wind & Fire got it all."

Maurice wasted no time in utilizing his newfound resources. He directed the group, its music, and its culture. This included, being the visionary on our album covers, finding our Japanese artist and other artists like Mati Klarwein, whom he found through the Miles Davis Group. Matthew did the *Last Days and Time* album cover, but Maurice used different ones. We were doing photographic covers: *Open Our Eyes* and *That's the Way of the World*, the standout cover with the black-and-white pictures by Norman Seeff. Norman had us jump and fall onto this queen-size mattress stack he had set up in his studio. He then superimposed those pictures on a white background. It defined our band's look and conveyed the energy of our music, becoming a memorable part of our visual identity.

Maurice wasn't just the founder of Earth, Wind & Fire. He was the architect. The visionary. The one who could see the finished painting before we'd even stretched the canvas.

He had strong ideas, yes—but not in the controlling sense. His ideas were *convictions*. Beliefs that shaped the core of who we were. He didn't just build a band. He built a philosophy. A culture. A mission.

And that mission was clear from day one: to create a group that was clean—in spirit, in sound, in life. Upbeat. Positive. Music with a message.

Not just in the lyrics—but in how we carried ourselves offstage. The point wasn't just to be entertainers—it was to be messengers, *musical healers*, representing something brighter in a world that could be very dark.

That was Maurice's canvas. And we all bought into that vision.

Almost always. There was one time—and only once—when I stepped outside the lines of that picture.

We were on tour. Preparing for a show, somewhere along the road—honestly, I don't even remember the city. They start to blur when you're in motion every night, sleeping in one state, waking in another. But I remember the moment.

We'd just wrapped sound check, and I was in my zone—quiet, focused, preparing mentally as I always did. That's when a band member came up to me. God rest his soul. He had this energy—playful, wild, always ready to *stir the pot a little*. He was our saxophonist and a character in the truest sense. He could make you laugh in a heartbeat and keep you guessing about what was coming next.

He walked over, leaned in with a mischievous grin, and said, *"Bro . . . guess what I got?"*

My face must've been blank because I didn't flinch. I wasn't in the mood for guessing games.

Then he dropped it.

"I've got some windowpane," he whispered.

I knew what that meant. LSD. Acid.

I'd never done it before. I wasn't drawn to that world. That just wasn't who I was—not personally, not musically, not spiritually.

But for whatever reason—and I still can't fully explain it—I just said, *"Yeah. Okay. Let's do it."*

There wasn't any buildup. No thinking it through. It was like the "yes" bypassed my mind and came straight from someplace I wasn't familiar with. Maybe I was curious. Maybe I was bored. Maybe I wanted to feel something different that night. I really don't know.

But we took it. And then, as always, it was showtime. I sat behind my kit, took a breath, waited for the lights to rise. And that's when things got . . . *weird*. The acid hit hard and fast.

Suddenly, the stage lights weren't just lights—they were *moods*. Entire emotional worlds. The deep blues and greens made me feel like I was being swallowed, like the drums were pulling me down into some underwater sadness. My spirit would *sink* right there under the spotlight, while my hands still kept moving.

Then, when the lights shifted—orange, yellow, hot reds—it was like someone threw open a window. *Boom*. Joy. Power. I'd jolt back to life and yell, *"Let's GO!"*

And that wave kept crashing back and forth—for the whole set. Up. Down. Up. Down. And through it all, in the middle of that swirling chaos, there was this . . . *voice* in my head. It wasn't an acid hallucination. It was my *inner voice*. My discipline. My training. My sense of duty as a drummer—the anchor of the band. It kept whispering, *"Whatever you do . . . don't speed up."* Then, *"Hold it. No, right there. Don't move. Wait. No. Okay. Yes. There. That's it. Right there. DON'T MOVE."* That mental conversation lasted the full hour and a half we were onstage. I was battling *myself*—the trippy ups and downs of the drug, the crowd's energy, the tempo, and the immense pressure to not let a single soul on that stage or in that crowd know what was going on inside me. I had to hold time like my life depended on it. I don't even remember how the show ended. I had been on the brink of collapse, but I kept the train on the tracks.

Years later, I shared the story with the band. They laughed, shook their heads, and looked at me like I'd just confessed to robbing a bank. And we all knew . . . *it never happened again.*

That was the first and last time I deviated from who we were. It wasn't just about the acid. It was about honoring the foundation Maurice built for us. We were Earth, Wind & Fire. We were joy. Discipline. Upliftment. Soul. We were about *the groove*, yes—but we were also about *intention*. We weren't a party band. We were a *purpose* band.

And stepping outside that—even once—showed me just how easy it is to lose that internal compass when you stop listening to it. How quickly one "yeah, okay" can turn into an identity crisis.

Maurice never lectured me about it. He didn't have to. His example was louder than any scolding could've been. Ten years older than most of us, he had life experience and musical depth we hadn't touched yet. He'd been through his fires. He knew where compromise led. And he knew exactly what it took to keep this thing we had built from *derailing.*

He wasn't just our band leader; he was our mentor, our coach, our *North Star.*

Maurice shared co-lead singing duties with vocalist Philip Bailey, and he wrote and co-wrote many of the songs like "Devotion," "Imagination," "Reasons," and "Sing a Song" that evolved into our distinctive sound. As a band, we were always chasing joy. Our brand of music emulated joy in its lyrics, its tone, its very being. And not the surface kind—the real thing. That feeling that hits you in the chest and lifts you two inches off the ground. That's what the foundation of Earth, Wind & Fire music was all about. That's what "*Sing a Song*" was built for.

I was riding my own personal groove. I fit right in with the Earth, Wind & Fire process. The guys accepted me right away. I was especially close to Verdine. If there were interviews to be done, we'd do them. It may have been easier because I wasn't the only new guy. Still coming on board were keyboardist Larry Dunn; saxophonist Andrew Woolfolk; flutist Ronnie Laws, who would go on to record on the first and his only album with us, *Last Days and Time*; rhythm guitarist Roland Bautista; and vocalists Bailey and Jessica Cleaves. I became fast friends with all my bandmates: We traveled together. We ate together. We were always around one another.

I hit my stride with these guys. They gave me something that I hadn't ever had in any other band, or, you know, they're helping me find something about myself that I know I want to stay with. I felt good about the chemistry within the group, which is very important. If you're in a group and the chemistry is not there, you might as well just pack it up and go home. The other thing was, I was so young that I had time to wait it out and give the Earth, Wind & Fire thing time to grow and see what it was going to evolve into. The group had two albums out with Warner Bros.; you could see where the music was or where the group was in its embryonic stages. But nothing is solidified because it takes time to build that chemistry. It's not just something that happens in one, two, three, or even ten rehearsals. When a group doesn't have chemistry, it's just a bunch of guys playing together, one big jam session. But when that chemistry happens, everybody's gelling, everybody's listening, and everyone complementing one another. And I made up my mind that I would stick it out and see what happens. I would give Earth, Wind & Fire some time.

Since we had just signed with CBS, we knew we were going to be going in the studio. It would have been stupid for me to leave at that point, right? So, we went in the studio and did *Last Days and Time* (1972). It was a good opening album; great tunes. We did a couple of covers: one was "Make It with You," by David Gates, which Bread made popular, and the other was "Where Have All the Flowers Gone?" the folk song written by Pete Seeger. The rest of it was original material. I was writing already back then, but I hadn't yet presented any material to the group. I had a writing partner, Douglas Gibbs, and during that period is when I wrote "Sounds Like a Love Song," which, much later, Jay-Z sampled.

In 1975, we shot up to a different level with our album *That's the Way of the World*. It was a standout record for us. Verdine says in interviews that it was our *What's Going On* album, referring to Marvin Gaye's album. We had great songs on *Last Days and Time* and *That's the Way of the World*. We had an album full of hits, including "Shining Star" and the title track. We got a lot of mileage out of that album. After that album we just kept climbing.

The guys in the group had great camaraderie. From the beginning, I knew what we had was extraordinary that would transcend everything else out there musically. Clive Davis had signed us to CBS to cut our first album, *Last Days and Time*. We were a band with a unique chemistry, and musically our sound combined jazz, R&B, African, and gospel. Maurice brought in producer Charles Stepney, and the music developed an even more distinctive flavor, as you would eventually hear in his classic composition and one of our theme songs, "That's the Way of the World." I loved watching this musical experiment evolve.

For my bandmates and me, it was all about the music. Back in the station wagon days (that's what I called them because we usually drove to our gigs in two older station wagons with all the luggage in the back), I was one of the designated drivers and loved driving for hours. The equipment truck followed us, driven by Bill Brown, our first roadie, and his assistant, Vanly de Lorenzo. We'd caravan through the countryside, and once we arrived at our venue, they'd set things up. Then, we'd hit the New York upstate area—Rochester, Buffalo, Syracuse, and those cities. During the station wagon days, we were doing the college circuit at enthusiastic colleges like Vassar.

In those early days, we were a band of brothers with lots of energy having fun with one another making music and living on the road. Larry Dunn and Andrew Woolfolk made the most mischief. If they were rooming together, they'd have water fights or throw water balloons. Larry would often stay up all night, and he was always ready to have some roguish fun. The most drama would be who was rooming with whom. Johnny might room with Verdine, Woolfolk with Larry, me and Al. If we didn't get our preferred roomies, we'd go to Leonard Smith, the road manager at that time, and he would work it out and get us checked in. We'd spend hours playing the game of chess. Larry and Andrew were the best players in the Earth, Wind & Fire League, but we were all competitive and loved to test one another.

I gravitated toward Al McKay in those early days because we had great conversations. He would talk about his previous experiences with the Watts 103rd Street Rhythm Band, Isaac Hayes, and the whole STAX thing. Al and I also talked about spirituality; we were searching, and we were open to all forms of getting in touch with ourselves. We were interested in exploring all channels of spirituality and talked about psychics and mediums. When rooming with guitarist Al McKay one night in our hotel room, I learned I could see auras. His bed was against a white wall, and I could see this glow. I'll never forget that glow.

These were good times of personal and professional growth. Maurice led by example in directing the mentality of the group. Maurice encouraged us to move beyond traditional categories of spirituality. For instance, he didn't subscribe to a particular "religion." His thinking was broader and bigger than that. He believed God was in everything. He encouraged us to explore all beliefs and systems to learn from them and to discover for ourselves the value in each of them.

Earth, Wind & Fire took off, and we were flying high in our early days. In 1974, we played the California Jam at the Ontario Motor Speedway with Emerson, Lake & Palmer, Black Oak Arkansas, Black Sabbath, the Eagles, and a ton of other acts. There were 300,000 people on this racetrack when we performed.

One of the most memorable performances for me was the first time we did an arena gig, at the Spectrum in Philly in 1973 with Gladys Knight and the Pips. It was the first time I ever heard 18,000 people scream "Aaaaahhhhh!" at the top of their lungs. Damn, what a feeling. I felt like I had, to a certain point, arrived—like I was a part of something that could turn out to be very special. I just had that kind of foresight.

Before we even did the Spectrum, we did the Uptown Theater, a small, renovated movie theater that held about 1,000 in downtown Philly, and that was another memorable performance. This was the beginning of the now-famous Earth, Wind & Fire theatrics. We were all standing in the wing, waiting to go onstage, and Maurice said, "This is what we're going to do when we go out there. When the curtains open, sit on the floor in yoga positions and stare at the audience. Don't do anything. Don't move. Just look at them." Maurice made no big speech; he just gave those directions. We knew what the set list was. We knew what we had to do.

And that's what we did for like ten minutes. We just froze in position onstage. It was awkward initially, but we won over the crowd when we started to play. That was the embryonic stage of where we would go with our showmanship and presentation.

It was apparent that our stage presence was evolving very quickly. Maurice didn't like the band just standing around onstage; he wanted to do something different, so he brought in magicians or a special effects person to help us create something unique onstage.

I understood Maurice wanted to push the envelope like that with this Black group, and stage theatrics would be our ticket. Our act kept evolving. Doug Henning was the first magician to work with us, and later David Copperfield. Magic act rehearsals were long and often complicated. Everything was about timing. Our magic acts never had any disastrous incidents but were crowd-pleasers that set us apart from our musical peers. After a successful show, we'd just retreat back to our hotel and hang out as musicians. There wasn't a whole lot of talk. We were off to the next thing, the next audience.

To be remembered, you must be unique and stand out from the crowd. Taking risks and trying new things can be essential to success in the music industry or any other field. However, it's necessary to balance risk-taking with careful planning and consideration of potential consequences. Being reckless or dangerous can harm you and others around you. I've learned to assess the risks and benefits before taking any action and always prioritize my safety and responsibility.

Our act was steadily coming together. I loved performing in the DMV area of Washington, DC, Maryland, and Virginia. Virginia is very beautiful to me, very green, and whenever we went down to Hampton, Virginia, we would play the Hampton Roads Coliseum. We were in Washington, DC, for the first time, playing at the DC Armory and playing cuts from one of my favorite albums at that time, 1972's *Last Days and Time*, our first album on CBS. Funkadelic was headlining the night, and we went out and did our thing. We felt good as we were ending with our last song. But even before we were finished, Funkadelic began to drown us out with their stomping groove, marching out from the restrooms in their exotic costumes, followed by a large cloud of smoke. The audience went wild and they just burned us right up. They totally outshined us. We learned the hard way that we weren't ready just yet. But we used it as motivation. When we returned home and rehearsed, we got tighter, and our showmanship began to gel. No other act ever stepped on us again.

In 1975, when we toured after releasing the album *Open Our Eyes*, an unforgettable opportunity arose. One of our special effects guys, who had worked in movies, came up with the idea of me doing a rotating drum stint in the middle of the air on that tour. It was like big scissors that tied into my drum seat and down into the platform so it would raise me up. We did this at the Hollywood Bowl when Herbie Hancock was on the bill when he had his *Head Hunters* album out. But this was my time to shine. I was the only contemporary musician doing something like this, so I relished in it for a few tours. We would close the show with the song "Mighty Mighty," with me rotating and playing the drums in the middle of the air. I was so concentrated on making sure I was keeping the tempo steady because when you're upside down, you're working against gravity, so your foot pedal, you're getting more resistance on that kick drum. Larry Dunn started doing the same thing on a big, spinning piano. This is when our special effects were in their early stages. Maurice wanted something different, not just a bunch of cats standing around the stage. He was open to whatever suggestions somebody could bring and wouldn't be too costly. We levitated Verdine. We'd bring him up to do a bass solo where he'd be sitting right next to a mic stand. We would come in, pick him up into a horizontal position, and he would stay there and keep playing. It was really quite simple. Verdine was wearing a jumpsuit, but inside the jumpsuit was a metal device, kind of like a ratchet wrench. As you pick it up, it would lock, lock, lock. We'd get it totally horizontal, and we could walk away because everything was locked in. But the audience didn't know that. They just saw Verdine kind of hanging out horizontally in the corner. We just had to make sure he was hooked up properly.

Then, there was the show we called the Tube show, where there were these nine giant, almost *Star Trek*–like tubes onstage at the Capital Centre, up on a platform. All you saw were nine tubes across the stage on the back of these risers. When our show would open, we'd have all this opening music, and the tubes would light up. Then, they'd go dark. And the next thing you knew, BANG! We were up inside the tube. What? The audience didn't know how that was done because the back of the stage was elevated, and we were down below on elevators. When the tubes went dark, we were moved up into the tubes. Lights came on. BANG! Everybody lost their minds with that simple trick. People still talk about the Tube show.

The magic acts worked out smoothly most of the time, but once we were on this steep incline, executing dance steps, and Maurice slipped and fell. Everyone on set gasped, but fortunately, after a few anxious seconds, he got back up and continued. We were cautious, courageous, calculating, and, yes, a little crazy.

Earth, Wind & Fire was on a roll and had no major problems because we had a sense of being on a mission. We knew we had something special. We were going through a period of musical evolution in the '70s. We didn't criticize one another, "Hey, you missed a beat there or this vocal was late." We just did our best to make our shows magical and highly entertaining. Sometimes, we'd get our fans up and dancing when we opened with "Power," a high-energy tune. We'd often include lesser-known songs from our early years like "Time Is on Your Side" and "Mom" from the *Last Days and Time* album. My head constantly swayed, watching my bandmates, communicating with them with my drum cadences, and keeping everyone in rhythmic sync. I'd watch the audience, their excitement feeding our energy. People would ask me what it was like to play the same songs night after night. I loved playing the hits because each song required every one of us in the group to maintain their part. But every now and then, we'd change from our preplanned set list. An audible would be called. We'd be scheduled to play "Can't Hide Love," but it would change to "Imagination," or "I'll Write a Song for You." It kept us on our toes, but no matter the song we played, we had to give each song its five minutes of fame every show, if we wanted to give the fans the show they came to see. And you could only do that by playing each part right.

It was 1975. We were riding a wave, but we weren't floating. We were *working*. We'd just come off our *That's the Way of the*

World tour, and the band was tight—tight in the way that only happens when you've sweated together for a hundred shows straight. Our live show had grown into a force. Not just sound. Not just light. *Experience.* By then, people didn't come to see us—they came to *feel* us. Maurice wanted to get pieces from all these different concerts, and he just took the best performances from each one. On *Gratitude,* you could really feel the energy. We were these young cats, and we were like full speed ahead, and you couldn't stop us. We felt like we were unstoppable.

That's when the idea came: Let's make a live album.

Maurice, as always, was thinking big. But his vision wasn't just about showcasing the show. It was about bottling energy. Capturing the pulse. Showing the world that Earth, Wind & Fire onstage was a different animal. More elastic. More alive. And so, the album *Gratitude* was born.

We recorded across multiple venues—Los Angeles, Chicago, Boston, St. Louis. Packed houses. Electricity in the air. We brought the best gear. Engineers who knew how to mic not just our instruments, but our *intention.* And every night we played, we knew: This wasn't just a gig. This was a stamp in time. But here's the twist. In the middle of all this raw, sweaty, improvisational *live* power, we dropped a few *studio tracks* into the mix, including "Sing a Song."

At first, it might've seemed like a contradiction—why put a fresh, polished studio cut on a live album? But that's the beauty of it. We weren't trying to document a tour. We were showing gratitude.

And what better way to express that than with a new song—something bright, bouncy, full of life?

"Sing a Song" was a celebration. Al McKay brought that signature guitar riff—tight, rhythmic, sunlit. Larry Dunn laid down those lush keys—simple but thick, like butter on warm bread. Verdine cooked up a bassline that *walked with a grin.* Charles Stepney produced as Maurice layered vocals with Phil, and the horns? Man, those horns didn't punch—they *danced.*

I knew my role: keep it steady, make it sing. I played it clean. Closed hi-hats, snappy snare, soft ride cymbal on the chorus. No frills. Just pulse. It wasn't about showing off—it was about *letting people feel good.* That was the purpose. The whole idea. "Sing a song . . . it'll make your day." Simple? Maybe. But profound when it's real. And so, when *Gratitude* was finalized, there sat "Sing a Song," smiling in the middle of it. Not loud. Not bragging. Just joyful. A gift.

We had to bring it *onstage.* So we did. Our first live performance of "Sing a Song" came shortly after the album dropped. I remember it vividly. San Diego Civic Arena. December 1975. The kind of crowd that didn't wait for the downbeat to start cheering. We hadn't played the song live before. Not fully. Not in front of people. That night, we were debuting it, fresh off the presses.

Now, you need to understand something: Trying out a new song live—especially a studio-perfect track like that—is risky. Audiences love what they know. But this song? We *knew* it would connect. You could feel it in the first four bars.

The lights dropped. The room buzzed. Then—BOOM. Al's guitar rang out, bright and crisp. I clicked in, tight. Snare, hi-hat, right on top of the beat, the way Maurice preferred it. "Sing a song . . ."

Maurice stepped to the front, smiling wide. He didn't sing *at* the crowd—he *invited* them. His voice was honey, warm and clear, sliding perfectly into the groove. The backup vocals rose like a chorus of sunlight behind him. Verdine was already moving like he was born to this beat. He played that bassline like it was second nature.

And the crowd? Man, they started swaying before the first verse was over. By the chorus, they were *singing it back.* I remember glancing over at Philip. He gave me this sideways grin like, *Yup. It's working.*

Halfway through, the horn section came in—blazing, joyful, tight as ever. They didn't just accent the groove. They *elevated* it. Trumpets stabbing the sky. Saxophones curling around the chords like smoke.

And me? I was in the pocket. Focused. Steady. Not trying to outshine anyone—just holding the mood. Every crash cymbal hit was like punctuation. Every rimshot timed to let the joy breathe.

People danced. People laughed. You could see shoulders drop, jaws loosen, arms lift. And that's when I understood the full *purpose* of the song. It wasn't just a track on an album. It was medicine.

We were a few years past Vietnam, but the country was still heavy. The Nixon era had left scars. Recession was creeping in. Cities were struggling. People were tired. And then here comes this song—four minutes of musical sunlight.

Maurice knew that. He always knew when the world needed something light but not shallow. Joy with roots.

So every time we played "Sing a Song" after that—whether in LA, London, or Tokyo—it became a *moment.* The horns would hit. The crowd would smile. We'd lean into the groove. And suddenly, we were all remembering something important: That joy is not naive. It's *necessary.*

People say music can't change the world. I don't know. But I do know it can change a room. And from there? Who knows.

Years later, I remember being backstage at the Montreux Jazz Festival. We were talking with some young musicians—bright, hungry cats from all over the globe. One of them asked, "Why did you put studio tracks on a live album?" Granted it was different at the time to mix live recordings with studio recordings on the same album. But we did it, one of the first groups to do so. Breaking creative ground as usual with studio tracks—"Celebration," "Can't Hide Love," and "Sing a Song"—that track carried the spirit of our live show even when there was no stage.

We still play the song today. And every time we do, I watch generations sing along—kids who weren't alive in the '70s, parents holding babies, couples dancing in the aisles.

So yes, "Sing a Song" wasn't captured in front of an audience for *Gratitude*, but it carried the spirit of one. It carried us. And we've been singing it ever since.

Every night we played, our music brought fans together and lifted them out of their everyday troubles. Earth, Wind & Fire elevated its audiences and transported them to another spiritual plane. Many of our fans have described our concerts as spiritual events. The closing number that night at the Capital

Centre in Washington, DC, in 1978 was "That's the Way of the World," and for some reason, the song moved people on a deeper emotional level, sparking a spiritual sensation that one doesn't usually feel at a concert. After the show, as he left the venue, Kenny Dickerson, a studio drummer who for years photographed Earth, Wind & Fire, told me that he continued to hear hundreds of people in the parking lot singing "That's the Way of the World" in harmonic unison. It wasn't just a small group of diehard fans. It was masses of people singing, total strangers loudly echoing the lyrics as they walked deep into the parking lot. Then and there, Kenny realized that Earth, Wind & Fire had a deep and lasting impact on people's lives on a spiritual level. He told me: "Earth, Wind & Fire touches the human spirit, and every time they walk out on that stage and sing the way they do, they are touching the human soul."

People constantly share how our music has positively impacted their lives. "We got married on 'Reasons' or 'September' was our wedding song because we got married on the 21st day of September." Or maybe they'll remind us, "Your music helped me get through this period in my life when I was going through this or that."

"Earth, Wind & Fire was some of the most memorable music in the soundtrack of our life."

"Man, my mother and father talk about you guys all the time. I grew up listening to your music."

We get these comments constantly. Every time we play, there's a new audience in the venue. It might be their first time seeing us live, so my job was not to disappoint them. Consistently giving your best is a key ingredient for success, whether in the form of a performance or how you approach your work or personal relationships. It's important to remember that each experience is unique and that every interaction provides an opportunity to impact others positively. I take the time and effort to give my best to help me achieve my goals and leave a lasting impression on those around me.

We were at the top of our game—no question about it.

Those mid-to-late '70s were like catching lightning in a bottle every single night, whether we were in the studio or onstage in front of twenty thousand people. The *music*, the *chemistry*, the *energy*—everything was on point. There was this collective momentum, a gravitational pull that swept us all into alignment. And when you're in that zone, that *sweet spot*, it's not about ego—it's about contribution. It's about excellence.

That was the Earth, Wind & Fire way.

Every rehearsal, every live set, every studio take—it had to matter. It had to be full-out.

Whether I was behind the kit during a sold-out arena show or laying down a groove during a 2 A.M. session at the Complex in West LA, my approach was always the same: Bring your best.

Back then, Fred White and I were playing the drums live together. That's not typical. You don't often see two drummers up there, side by side, making it work without stepping on each other's feet. But just like I saw it done with James Brown live as a child back in the '60s, we made it work—beautifully.

Fred had that deep-pocket backbeat. His style was solid, rooted, unshakable. He knew how to keep that 2 and 4 crisp, locked in, no nonsense. He held the groove. That was

Fred. And that's what Maurice loved about him—consistency, clarity, the kind of playing you could build skyscrapers on.

Me? I was drawn to a different flavor.

I came up on big band swing, and I carried that into our funk. I was all about fills and accents, coloring in the edges of the beat, shaping the feel of a track beyond just timekeeping. I brought that percussive freedom, that jazz-informed lift. I wasn't reckless—I was disciplined, absolutely—but I allowed myself more expression inside the rhythm.

And slowly, at first—but then more boldly—I took that freedom.

That's the thing about Earth, Wind & Fire. There was structure, yes. But within that structure was a world of possibility, and if you had something to say with your instrument, there was room to say it.

The foundation for that freedom was built years earlier. Back when I was just a young drummer hustling gigs down at Maverick's Flat, the legendary soul club in LA, I was cutting my teeth in front of some of the toughest, sharpest crowds you could play for. If you weren't bringing it, they'd let you know real fast.

And I was studying hard, too. I took lessons at Grant's Music Center, which at the time was a hub for Black musicians. That place had an energy. It was the closest thing to a conservatory that reflected *our* sound, *our* rhythm, *our* culture. That's where I started learning how to swing with a full band—brass, woodwinds, rhythm, the works.

So by the time we hit that *Gratitude* period?

I was ready.

You can hear it on that album. That live energy. That electricity we captured and bottled on wax. It wasn't just a live record—it was a moment in history. And it still holds up because it wasn't artificial. There was no pretense. That was who we were—raw, real, in our prime.

I was playing all the live shows then, before I eventually transitioned more into a front-of-stage role as a vocalist. But in the studio, Maurice, Fred, and I shared drum duties. It was a rotating wheel, not a competition. Maurice had a keen ear—he knew what style of playing each song called for, and he wasn't sentimental about it. If a track needed Fred's straightforward, unshakeable pulse, Fred got the call. If it needed something jazzier, more nuanced, or dynamically layered—that might be me.

Sometimes I *wanted* to be on more studio tracks. I won't lie. I had ideas. I had feel. But I respected Maurice's decisions. That's what it took to be part of a band that great. You had to check your ego. Maurice was the visionary, and the late, great Charles Stepney brought that producer's finesse to albums like *Open Our Eyes*, *That's the Way of the World*, and *Gratitude*. Together, they sculpted the sound.

And the rest of us? We executed.

We didn't fight the process. We trusted it.

Everything just seemed to click back then. The arrangements, the vocals, the musicianship—it was like a puzzle coming together with every new project.

I don't remember reading a single bad review during that stretch. Not one.

Critics were on our side. Fans were locked in. Musicians were studying us. Everyone in the band was *fired up* about what the other guys were doing. There was respect in the room. And when Maurice was happy? You knew you were doing something right.

But I wasn't just growing as a drummer—I was growing as a musician.

I began to understand the theatrics of performance. Not the kind you fake—I'm talking about the *discipline* of keeping the audience in the palm of your hand. Once that curtain rises and you engage that crowd—you don't break character. Ever. You maintain the illusion. You hold the spell.

Because here's the deal: Once you lose the audience, once you break the magic, it's hard—*real hard*—to get it back. You've got to be flawless in your transitions, your pacing, your connection. You have to respect the audience's attention.

That's why sound checks matter so much. They're not just for tuning instruments or checking mics. They're the final brushstrokes before the canvas is unveiled. You check your intros, your outros, your lighting cues, your graphics, your timing. You make sure every part of that show is seamless.

Because if a screen glitches mid-set or a mic cuts out during a solo, it pops that bubble you worked so hard to inflate.

And then people go:

"Damn . . . they *had* me."

That's the heartbreak—*they had you*. Past tense.

We worked too hard to let that happen. So we rehearsed relentlessly, we polished endlessly, and we held ourselves to a standard that very few bands could match. That's how we kept our edge. That's how we stayed *tight.*

That's where we were as a group.

And the best part? We weren't doing it because of some corporate mandate or marketing gimmick. We were doing it because we *loved* it. Because we felt like we were *a part of something bigger* than ourselves.

Every night we hit the stage, we weren't just performing. We were *lifting spirits.* We were spreading joy, speaking in a language that cut across race, class, borders, and generations.

That's what Earth, Wind & Fire has always been about. From behind the kit or standing under the spotlight, from that first studio session to the final bow of a tour—our mission has never changed: *Bring your best. Play with heart. Never break the magic.*

During this time, there were no scandals, no bickering. We avoided over-the-top egos, drug addictions, and money problems. Still, we were young men, and young men have egos. But astronomical success has a way of unraveling even the most sturdy of foundations. And things started to change for us as we became more and more successful. Our saxophonist, Ronnie Laws, left the group shortly after the *Last Days and Time* album. He dreamed of being a solo artist and made those dreams come true with nineteen solo albums and a reputation as an acclaimed jazz musician.

Eventually, Al McKay would leave. Al was a great musician and a fine songwriter. He wrote many songs along with Maurice and other bandmates. He's credited with "September," "Saturday Nite," "Sing a Song," "Best of My Love," and

"Flowers" by The Emotions, and many others. He contributed significantly to the sound of Earth, Wind & Fire. However, the relationship between Maurice and Al slowly and steadily began to erode. Since Al had already led bands before he joined Earth, Wind & Fire, he didn't see himself under Maurice, and he thought he could be in a better situation. When we were in Buenos Aires, Argentina, for a performance, Al said to me, "I'm out."

I replied: "Al, find the change you seek."

He would soon leave the group and start his own Earth, Wind & Fire Experience with the Al McKay All-Stars.

The changes in Earth, Wind & Fire led me to reflect on my own life. My career and the group's success weren't the only things I focused on. I had never intended to remain single throughout my life, but while I met many women, I didn't meet anyone who had the spiritual qualities I was looking for; I was continually searching for the right person for me. I wasn't looking for someone who wanted to be married to the image of Earth, Wind & Fire, and I wasn't looking for someone who was interested only in herself. I was looking for someone independent, someone who would be a good homemaker, someone who came from a good family, someone I could love and who would love me. I was looking for that "forever love" from someone who understood it, saw it growing up, and cherished it.

In 1977, I met Susie, who worked at a Family Savings and Loan Bank on Crenshaw and Exposition. I often went down to Lindbergh Nutrition, a health food store that was farther south down the street, to eat, and then head to the bank to take care of business. Susie was sitting at her desk. I saw her and was intrigued right away.

I did the 'ol double take, walked up to her, and confidently said, "Could I have your number?"

Surprisingly, without missing a beat, she said, "I'll take your number instead."

I recovered smoothly and replied, "Cool."

About two weeks later, she called. We connected to see the movie *Star Wars* at Grauman's Chinese Theater in Hollywood. It was perfect. We were both into the sci-fi genre. As we spent time together, what I saw in her was her vibrant personality and a big smile. She was beautiful and very easy to be around. Back then, astrology was the happening thing. I asked what her sign was. She said Taurus. I was Cancerian, and so it was a match there. We had so much in common. We'd go on exciting dates like the drag strip races as we were both car people.

Susie and I started dating in 1977. In 1979, and without fanfare, while we were at dinner having a casual conversation in a sushi bar on Wilshire Boulevard called Tokyo (how appropriate since my favorite place outside the United States is Japan), I asked her to marry me.

Without hesitation, she said, "Yes."

I've always believed that a good marriage isn't built on grand gestures or perfect compatibility—it's built on respect, communication, shared interests, and a sense of humor. And if you're lucky, it's built day by day, with someone who's just as willing as you are to show up and do the work—not just when it's easy, but when it's hard.

First, let me talk about respect—because without it, love starts to feel like an obligation instead of a choice.

To me, respect means more than saying "yes, dear" or pulling out a chair. It's about honoring your partner's mind. Their autonomy. Their silence. It's about knowing that even when you disagree, you don't diminish each other. You *listen*, even when you're tired. You show up, even when you're frustrated. You give them the same patience you'd want for yourself.

I've always tried to treat Susie as my equal—not because the world told me to, but because I saw her from the very beginning as someone whole, with her own gifts, ideas, and rhythm. And she's treated me the same. Even in the chaos of life in the music industry, she never tried to change me or clip my wings. She gave me space to be *me* while still keeping us grounded as *we*.

Communication is the next cornerstone—and that's not just about talking. It's about *listening with intent.* It's about understanding not just the *words* someone says, but the *feelings underneath them.*

Some of our most meaningful conversations haven't been long, dramatic heart-to-hearts. Sometimes they're just a hand on the shoulder after a long day. A look across the room that says, "I got you." Or the simple act of asking, "How are you really doing?"—and actually sticking around to hear the answer.

When conflict does come—and it always does in any real relationship—communication is the bridge that gets you back to each other. I don't believe in silent treatments. I don't believe in punishment disguised as patience. I believe in *working through things with love.* No scoreboard. No ego. Just a mutual desire to understand and heal.

And then there are shared interests. Now, let's be real: You don't have to do *everything* together. That's not healthy either. But having passions that intersect—music, art, travel, culture, even just taking walks together—creates *touch-points* of joy that keep you connected. It means you're not just surviving side by side; you're actually enjoying each other's company.

Susie and I both appreciate the arts—she has an incredible eye. She helps me see beauty in places I might've missed. Whether it's walking through a gallery in Tokyo, picking out a piece of sculpture, or discussing a film over dinner, there's a creative current that flows between us. That matters.

Finally, I think a sense of humor is essential. Not because marriage is a joke—but because life can be heavy. And if you can't laugh—at yourself, at the absurdity of it all, at the small mishaps and missed exits—then you're missing one of the greatest tools for survival.

There have been times when the only thing that brought us back from the edge was a laugh. A knowing smile. A joke that only the two of us would get. That kind of humor is intimate. It's not about being funny—it's about being *safe enough* to be silly. To not take everything so seriously that you forget you're still *alive* together.

You know, people sometimes look at a long marriage and assume it's smooth sailing. That once you've made it past year ten, year twenty, or year thirty, you're on autopilot.

That's not the truth. A long marriage is like a long tour: There are cities you love and cities that drain you. There are nights where the sound is perfect and nights where everything feels off. But if you trust each other, if you keep showing up, tuning the instruments, and staying in rhythm with one another—you can create something *timeless.*

It's knowing that both of you will change—and choosing, over and over again, to grow in parallel. To remain curious about the person across the table. To *keep discovering* each other, year after year.

That's what Susie and I have. And that's what I hope for anyone who sets out on that journey. Because when you find someone who truly sees you, respects you, communicates with you, shares joy with you, and can still make you laugh when life turns serious—that's more than love. That's a *partnership.*

And I wouldn't trade that for anything.

For all the right reasons, Susie and I married at my home in Sherman Oaks on Encanto Drive in a small wedding with immediate friends and family. No one was opposed to Susie's union with me. My bandmates supported me doing my thing, though I wouldn't be surprised if some wondered how any woman would handle being a part of Earth, Wind & Fire during our prime. Yet Susie was very independent and self-reliant, so she didn't need me to hold her hand.

Susie enjoyed attending shows from time to time in those early years. She would come backstage, sometimes watching the show from the wings. I was excited for her to see what I was doing and what I was accomplishing.

I was only home a few weeks after our wedding before I was back on tour. We didn't have much discussion about my musician's lifestyle. We naturally fell into "our thing" and had a flow. It never came up in our marital talks that she was uncomfortable or was facing things she didn't think would work out. Our marriage was smooth, and Susie and I were having a ball. We had our first child, John-Ralph, on September 12, 1982. Having a child didn't change us, but something was about to happen that would rock my entire world as I knew it.

Part Two

WIND

Chapter 4

HUMILITY AND FORGIVENESS

Ralph Johnson is a person who thinks deeply about life and the universe and what's happening around us. He is inquisitive, a deep thinker, and an intellectual. As a performer, he is curious about how music connects to other forms of life and thinking deeply about how it plays into the universe.

—Rev. Michael Livingston, childhood friend

Earth, Wind & Fire was sitting on top of the world as the 1980s dawned. We were one of the biggest music groups in the world, coming off a series of highly awarded albums including *That's the Way of the World*, *Spirit*, and *I Am*. Top-ten hits such as "Shining Star," "Boogie Wonderland," "Fantasy," and "After the Love Has Gone" were blaring over radio stations everywhere, and we sold out concerts all over the world. It couldn't get much better.

During the late 1970s and early 1980s, we stepped into an entirely new chapter of our career when we began making music videos. At the time, videos weren't just promotional tools—they were becoming an art form of their own. MTV was changing the landscape, and suddenly music wasn't only something people heard; it was something they *saw.* For us, that visual element elevated our music to another level and helped us reach an even wider audience, including people who might not have discovered us through radio alone.

One of the videos that really stands out in my memory is for the song "Magnetic." We filmed it at the Bradbury Building in downtown Los Angeles, which is this incredible, historic landmark with ornate ironwork, towering light-filled atriums, and an atmosphere that feels cinematic the moment you walk in. The setting alone gave the video a sense of mystery and drama. The concept leaned toward a futuristic, almost post-nuclear theme—something edgy and forward-thinking that matched the mood of the music. It felt like we were stepping into a world that existed slightly ahead of its time.

What I remember most vividly, though, was the director. The video was directed by a cat named Jay Dubin, who was already well known for his work directing high-end television commercials. Those commercials had a polish, style, and visual confidence that really set them apart, and it honestly knocked me out that we were able to get someone of his caliber to direct our video. At that moment, it felt like a validation—not just of the song, but of where we were creatively as a band. We weren't just making videos; we were collaborating with top-tier visual artists who took our music seriously.

Another favorite of mine is the video for "Thinking of You," and that one stands out for completely different reasons. The entire theme had a distinctive, elegant vibe, and for reasons that still make me smile, we cast a lot of Japanese models. That resonated with me personally, because I already had a deep appreciation for Japan after traveling there about ten years earlier. There was something about the aesthetics, the grace, and the overall sensibility that felt like a natural fit for the song.

The look of the band in that video was also a turning point. For the first time, we were all dressed in suits. Up to that point, our visual style had always been expressive and experimental, but this was different—it was sharp, refined, and confident. Those suits gave us a whole new presence on-screen. We looked polished and grown, like we were stepping fully into our maturity as artists. When I watch that video now, I still feel that sense of pride, because it captured not just a song, but a moment when everything—music, image, and identity—came together just right.

The first video we did, however, was of "Boogie Wonderland," but I distinctly remember playing it live at the Forum. Los Angeles. My city. My heartbeat. My origin.

You never really leave the place where your rhythm started. The streets may change. Skylines shift. But the pulse—that early groove that shaped your footsteps—stays with you. And when we played "Boogie Wonderland" in

LA, especially at the height of our powers, it wasn't just another gig on the map. It was a full-circle moment. It was coming home.

There's something magnetic about the Forum in Inglewood. That building holds ghosts and fireworks. It's where the Lakers built a dynasty. Where the Stones, Zeppelin, and Prince made walls sweat. But for me? It's where my parents sat in the audience, smiling in their Sunday best. It's where I saw my son, barely tall enough to see over the seat in front of him, watching his dad descend from a cosmic planet pod onto the stage. And it's where "Boogie Wonderland" turned into a kind of sacred chaos—a glitter-drenched, high-octane celebration that burned through the building like a disco-funk wildfire.

It was the late '70s. Al McKay was producing this new piece for another group under Maurice's production company. Maurice heard it and wanted to do it, and he called in the Emotions to do the background. "Boogie Wonderland" dropped like a meteor. That collaboration with The Emotions—man, it had a life of its own. That joint didn't just groove—it *exploded*. The horns punched like brass fireworks. The bassline didn't walk—it *strutted*. And the beat? That beat was a locomotive, and I was driving. On this particular night at the Forum, the air buzzed with anticipation. People weren't just ready to party. They were ready to *lose themselves*. Disco was alive, and while "Boogie Wonderland" was our first and only foray into disco music, we were riding that groove like it was eternal. It wasn't intentional, but boy, were we happy it turned into a big hit.

I caught a glimpse of the crowd just before we went on. You ever see 17,000 sequins shimmer at once? That's what it looked like. People dressed to *boogie*—platform shoes, butterfly collars, glitter everywhere. It looked like someone had shaken a giant snow globe full of funk.

Backstage, I had my usual pre-show rhythm. Stretch the wrists. Breathe. Tap out the opening kick pattern on my thighs. We were well into the show already, but I always saved a special gear for "Boogie Wonderland." That song asked everything of me. Drummers know: That groove *doesn't let up*. Four-on-the-floor with a funky overlay, tight hi-hat work, relentless back beat—it's a workout, man. A cardio class with cymbals.

Verdine was bouncing in place, bass strapped high, ready to jump out of his shoes. Larry was grinning behind the keys. Phil gave me that look—the one that said, "Let's blow the roof off."

And then Maurice gave the cue.

The lights dropped. The stage glowed orange and purple, like a late-night sun was rising just for us. A fog machine hissed, covering the floor in smoke. Out in the crowd, you could feel people perk up like their souls just sat up straighter.

The first note hit. BAM—horns. Tight. Sharp. Then that rhythm guitar lick—Al McKay, clean as polished chrome.

"Dance, boogie wonderlaaaand . . ."

And the Forum *erupted*. It was like someone opened a bottle of fizzy funk and shook it too hard. People jumped to their feet, arms in the air, bodies already locked into the pulse. That first chorus turned the arena into a single living creature—sweating, shouting, shimmering.

Playing that groove live was a lesson in stamina. It wasn't flashy. It wasn't a showboat drummer's dream. But it was precise. Relentless. And full of joy. Every limb had to work in sync. Kick driving forward. Snare keeping people on the two and four. Hi-hat sizzling just enough to keep the rhythm dancing. But you couldn't just *play* "Boogie Wonderland." You had to *believe* it. You had to move like it mattered.

The Emotions came out from stage left—Jeanette, Wanda, and Sheila—dressed in mirrorball magic, voices sharper than diamonds. Their energy added rocket fuel to the song. When they hit the line, "Midnight creeps so slowly into hearts of men," the whole building leaned forward. Those ladies didn't sing backup—they sang fire.

And Maurice? He was *commanding*. Tall, steady, eyes lit with fire, he held the stage like a high priest of funk. Every gesture—precise. Every line—punched with meaning.

Phil and I would lock eyes now and then. Between hits. Between fills. Just a glance to say, "This is working." Sometimes we'd even grin, like two kids who snuck into a party and found out they were the main event.

I'll never forget this moment mid-song. We were deep in the groove—second chorus, crowd roaring—and suddenly I saw a man in the second row stand up on his seat, jacket off, tie undone, spinning it over his head like a helicopter. His whole section *followed*. It was like a chain reaction of joyful anarchy. That's what "Boogie Wonderland" did to people. And we gave it back.

I added a slight shift to the hi-hat—opened it up just a little on the offbeat. Nothing drastic. But enough. Larry caught it and responded with a clavinet riff that danced over the top like static electricity. Verdine nodded—he was listening. That's the thing about live music: Even when the song's the same, the moment never is. Every night, we built that Wonderland from scratch.

Now the audience was *with* us. Not just singing. *Chanting.* Screaming it like a rally cry. Hands clapping in sync with the beat. Thousands of bodies riding the rhythm like it was the last night on Earth. But I wasn't tired. I was *alive.*

That's the gift of a song like "Boogie Wonderland." It gives you *energy.* The more you put in, the more it gives back. It's like playing inside a storm that's made of glitter and joy.

In the final chorus, the lights went wild. Spotlights spinning. Lasers hitting the disco ball above, casting a universe of tiny stars across the ceiling and crowd. The whole Forum became a galaxy. A literal wonderland. And in that last push, we went full throttle.

And then—BAM. Final hit. Then came the roar. You don't forget that sound. It's not just noise. It's gratitude. It's release. It's people saying, "You gave us joy, and we're giving it right back."

I stood behind my kit, chest heaving. I looked out into the crowd and found one face—my mother. Grace Johnson. In a light blue blouse, hands clapping above her head, smiling with her whole being. My dad beside her, standing straight, pride written in every crease of his brow.

That . . . that was it for me. Not the fame. Not the gold records. *That* moment. My parents, in the crowd, in my city, watching their son help create joy. After the show, we came offstage glowing. No one said much at first. We didn't need to. You feel when it clicks. When the music doesn't just land—it *lives.*

Later that night, I drove through LA with the windows down, breeze against my face, still humming the groove. I passed the blocks I grew up on. Hobart Boulevard. Eighth and Ninetieth. The neighborhoods that shaped my hands, my discipline, my ears. The sidewalks that first heard me tapping out rhythms with pencils and drumsticks. I thought about that eight-year-old kid who once got a snare drum for Christmas. Who used to dream about playing the Forum. Who once stood in line with his father at the Southern California Music Company, heart racing just to touch a cymbal.

Now here I was. Driving home from the Forum after playing one of the biggest hits of our career. In front of a sold-out crowd. Five times. In my hometown. *That's* "Boogie Wonderland." It's not just a song. It's not just a party. It's a disco-flavored *homecoming.* And every time I hear it—even now—I see those lights. I feel that floor. I hear the stomp of 17,000 pairs of feet. And I remember: That night, we didn't just play a concert. We opened a portal. And for a few shining minutes, LA danced inside it.

We were riding high. There's no other way to say it. At that point, Earth, Wind & Fire wasn't just successful—we were *on fire*. The albums were selling. The tours were selling out. The music was everywhere. Radio, television, award shows, stadiums. We were traveling the world and being embraced like royalty. There was a feeling—unspoken, but shared—that this thing we had built together was still climbing, still expanding, still reaching for something even bigger.

But even with all this success, I never forgot family. My sister Pam will tell the story at family gatherings of how, when she was a teenager, we were going to play at the Hollywood Palladium. She asked me if she could invite some of her girlfriends to the show.

As she giddily started sharing the names one by one, I looked at her and said, "How many friends you got there, Pam? Half of LA?"

"But my brother came through and I felt like royalty walking in with my excited friends. I felt like a movie star and most importantly, like my family put me first. That's what my brother Ralph did."

Naturally, I too assumed that with success, greater unity would come to my Earth, Wind & Fire family. The tighter the spotlight became, the closer we'd all draw together as a band. That's how it's *supposed* to work, right? You win together. You celebrate together. You grow together.

Neither I—nor anyone else in the band—expected what came next.

I remember that moment as clearly as if it happened yesterday.

It was 1982 when word came down that Maurice wanted to call a meeting. His sister and administrative assistant, Geri, reached out and told us we were all to gather at The Complex in West Los Angeles—our home base, where our recording studios were housed. So when the call came, none of us felt alarmed.

In fact, it was the opposite. As we started arriving that afternoon, the mood was casual—almost light. Guys were joking in the hallway. A few of us were talking about upcoming tour dates, new music ideas, business possibilities. With our popularity still surging and our reputation flourishing, it felt natural to assume this meeting was a *celebration*. Maybe Maurice wanted to toast the journey so far. Maybe there was a new vision to share. A new chapter to unveil.

We even joked about the catering. That's how confident we were. How secure things felt. But as we filtered into the room and took our seats, something shifted. The energy wasn't what we expected.

There were no smiles waiting for us. No champagne. No sense of anticipation or triumph. The room felt . . . heavy. Still. Like the air had thickened without anyone touching a thermostat.

Maurice entered the room. He wasn't pacing. He wasn't animated. He was calm—*too* calm. Centered in that way he got when something serious was coming. His presence always commanded respect, but that day it carried a different weight. A gravity I'd never felt from him before.

As I looked around the room—at men I'd spent years sweating beside onstage, men who had become brothers in every sense except blood—I could see it on their faces too.

Confusion. Curiosity. A creeping sense that maybe we had misread the moment.

Maurice waited until everyone was in the room. No small talk. No warm-up. Then he spoke.

And just like that, the illusion cracked.

What followed wasn't a meeting. It wasn't an announcement. The best way I can describe it now—looking back with the benefit of time—is that it felt like the Last Supper. Not in drama. In symbolism. A gathering of people who didn't yet know how profoundly things were about to change, even though the change was already standing in the room with us.

I remember sitting there, listening, but also watching.

Watching shoulders slump. Watching eyes drop. Watching people shift in their chairs as reality set in. The future we'd assumed was unfolding in a straight line, suddenly bent sharply to the side.

For me, it felt like time slowed down.

Maurice, without hesitation, spoke curtly. "Look, here's what's going on. I'm taking a break. I'm going to do a solo album, and it looks like Phil will do one too. You guys can do what you want. Maybe we will come back together; maybe we won't." In true Maurice White style, there was no beating around the bush or sugarcoating the message. He was a straight shooter. His voice had no attitude, no anger, just firmness. "So, that's what's going down."

There was dead silence. That was it. There was no warning. Maurice didn't take any questions, and there was no discussion. His message came out of nowhere. It's not like he said,

"In ninety days, I'm cutting this thing off, so get prepared." The emphatic finality of his words still rings in my head: "This is what I'm doing. You guys are on your own."

That always bothered me. My relationship with Maurice was fine up to that point. We got along great and I revered him as a mentor. But you just can't call a meeting at this particular time to do what he did the way he did it. You can't tell us after we've been touring that we're going to just stop this whole thing, and we've had no time to prepare for the stop, right? Right? Exactly. In less than thirty minutes, it was over. I was like, "Damn man, come on. Warning, a month, two months, six months, if this was the plan." My issue was always the way it was done.

All of us were in shock as we listened to Maurice talk and after he left the room.

I wasn't angry. Not yet. I wasn't scared. Not exactly. What I felt most was disorientation. Like standing on a familiar stage and realizing the floor beneath you had subtly moved.

This was Earth, Wind & Fire. We weren't supposed to fracture. We weren't supposed to pause. We were built on momentum. On unity. On vision.

That meeting marked the end of one era and the uncertain beginning of another. We didn't all leave the room changed immediately—but something fundamental had shifted. The unspoken certainty that *tomorrow would look like today* was gone.

As we filed out afterward, there was no laughter. No joking. Just quiet nods. People lost in their own thoughts. Each of us carrying the weight of what we'd just heard, unsure how to set it down.

I walked out into the Los Angeles sunlight that afternoon feeling like the ground had tilted slightly—not enough to knock you over, but enough to make you check your footing.

We didn't know then how long the ripple from that meeting would last. We didn't know what it would demand of us—emotionally, creatively, spiritually. All we knew was that the path forward was no longer clear. Success prepares you for applause—but it doesn't prepare you for change.

That day at The Complex taught me something I would carry for the rest of my life: That even at the highest peaks, you have to be ready for the ground to shift beneath you. And when it does, the only thing that matters is how you stand in that moment—steady, honest, and willing to face what comes next.

I felt like I was in a *Star Wars* movie right before that last battle when the characters invoke the protective phrase: "May the force be with you." I knew I had to figure out what all this meant for me. I didn't have a solo deal in place like he and Phil did.

I couldn't believe what Maurice had just told the band. I didn't talk to anyone after the meeting, not Verdine, not Larry, not Al, no one. I just couldn't wrap my mind around it. "Did he really just do that? Come on, Reece," I said to myself. I sat in silence in my Porsche 911, trying to figure out what to do. The word of the day was "Damn." None of us were expecting this. There were no telltale signs before this meeting that any of this was going to happen. We had just released our latest album, *Raise!*, a few months prior in 1981, and it was another hit anchored by the song “Let’s Groove.” But nothing lasts forever. Not even greatness.

Our studio manager Richie Salvato recalled to me about that time: “How devastating was this moment? Band members were receiving road money, and that was gone . . . They had exclusive homes and fancy cars, but suddenly, their income stream was cut off. Many lost their cars and flashy lifestyles. They lost homes and had to move into apartments. Some got divorced. It wasn’t easy.”

Once I arrived home, I shared with Susie what had happened. We had assets; we had money saved. I told her that we’d just have to figure some things out. She looked at me as if to say, “I know you got this. I trust you.” This was a challenging moment at the beginning of a tough period in life, one I figured would last no more than a few months. Philip would say the band broke up. I said it was going to be a short hiatus. I’d be proven wrong.

A few months later, Al McKay and I went to our label, CBS, and tracked down Larkin Arnold, the savvy and influential Black A&R executive. We told him what happened in our meeting with Maurice. Although I knew Larkin would be able to help us, his response confirmed the brutality of the music business.

“We’ve got Maurice.” He grinned. “We’ve got Philip.” He looked us straight in the eye and unashamedly asked, “What do you have?” Larkin made his point clearly: The label still had the marquee names in the group under contract. The rest of us were on our own. We learned in that moment that we had nothing. I was in disbelief. Attitudes and perceptions about Maurice were changing for me. Not significantly, but they did change.

When I reflected on what had happened, I thought that maybe Maurice was just burned out or that maybe he felt he could have a great solo career like Lionel Richie, who broke away from the Commodores and had done exceptionally well. I think Maurice also thought he could do well as a solo artist. He did put out an eponymous album, *Maurice White*, that included a remake of "Stand by Me" because Ben E. King, who sang the original version, was his friend. He thought it would be a hit, but the album didn't go anywhere. It's possible CBS didn't promote the album as fully as they would have promoted an Earth, Wind & Fire album, or it's possible that audiences weren't ready for a Maurice White solo album without the members of Earth, Wind & Fire. Whatever the reasons, Maurice's solo album fell flat.

Around the same time that Maurice's album failed to attract attention, Phil did the *Chinese Wall* album that Phil Collins produced. I was fortunate to have a song on that album called "Go" that Marcel East and I co-wrote. Marcel's brother Nate played bass on the album, so he presented the tune to Phil, and he added it to the album. The album went gold, and the single "Easy Lover" was a Billboard Hot 100 No. 2 hit. Having my song included on the album was a financial balloon for a moment. Phil eventually moved back to Denver and cut a few well-received gospel albums.

As time passed, other band members started doing production gigs or writing and playing with others. I had stayed in contact with our keyboardist Larry Dunn more than anyone else in the band. He cut an album, the *Larry Dunn Orchestra*, and asked me to play drums on it. Then, in 1983, Motown asked Al McKay if he would produce the Temptations' next album. I was at Al's house in Los Feliz, and he said, "Slick," the nickname they used to call me back then, "you want to help me produce the Temptations on Motown?"

I replied, "Are you serious? Yeah, I'd love to." I was so thankful that Al asked me to participate. We put "our foot in it" as co-producers. Otis Williams, the group's founding member, would always say that *Truly for You* was one of the greatest albums they had ever done, and the single from the album, "Treat Her Like a Lady," proved to be a big hit for them. Honing my producing skills on this album—as well as working with Al McKay as producer and the Mighty Tempts as artists—was one of the most incredible experiences I'd ever had in music. As a writer and singer, I am in the service of the song, but when I stepped behind the boards as a producer, I was looking for the sound that best served the song. How would this song sound if we changed the tempo on the chorus? What if the singer held back a beat on the introductory verse? What sounds would turn the song into one that would give listeners a chance to hear some new sound, or to listen to music in a new way, or simply to determine which singles would drive people to the record store. As a producer, I also was the one who would determine which song made the cut and was included on an album, or which songs might be just the right song for a singer and the singer's voice. As a producer, I now had the opportunity to shape an artist's sound, and an artist's sound becomes that artist's identity.

After the success of producing the Temptations album and writing a song for Phil's *Chinese Wall* album and, I believed other projects would be on the horizon. Somehow, I'd get through this period, even though I didn't realize how long this break from the group might last. As one year turned to two, and two dragged into three, my music opportunities soon dried up. To complicate matters, the group was embroiled in a fierce legal battle with CBS over royalties, so publishing income paused. During these six years, I was bitter. This whole breakup or hiatus left me with bad feelings toward Maurice. Every day I thought, "How could you do this, Reece?"

Susie was pregnant with our first child—our son John-Ralph. In the middle of touring, rehearsals, studio work, and the constant rhythm of life with Earth, Wind & Fire, this was *real life* pressing in: bills, diapers, responsibility, love wrapped in total vulnerability. That was added pressure.

I knew right then—before he took his first breath—that I needed to generate consistent income, and I could no longer rely on music. Not yet again. Not in the way I needed to support a growing family. I needed options—*stable* ones.

So I picked up the phone and called a friend, Tony Chargois.

Tony owned US Mechanical, a company deeply involved in construction, plumbing, and fire protection systems—a blue-collar world far removed from stages and spotlight. I told him, "Tony . . . I need to work. Can I come work with you?"

His answer was instantaneous.

"Yes."

Just like that. No hesitation. No judgment. Just a lifeline. Suddenly . . . my life took a different trajectory. Tony didn't just give me a job. He gave me a craft. He taught me how to cut pipe. How to thread it. How to hang it. How to build something sturdy, something physical, something that would stand up to gravity and pressure.

He put me on a massive contract—installing the fire protection system for the Sports Club in West Los Angeles, at Santa Monica and Sepulveda Boulevards. Every morning, I'd wake up early, slip into my jeans and T-shirt, cinch on a tool belt, and step into a world where the soundtrack was power tools and clanging steel.

It was tiring. It was tedious. It was *brutally hard work.*

But every inch of that building? I hung it. I took pride in that.

For about three years, I lived in that reality—hands wrapped around wrenches, sweat on my brow, the sun rising before my day and setting after it. Tony taught me more than plumbing. He taught me perseverance, dignity in honest work, and the quiet pride that comes from building something strong with your own hands.

Tony is no longer with us. But his generosity saved my life, not just financially, but spiritually. And I still carry those skills with me—not to install fire lines anymore, but to remind myself I *can* build, I *can* adapt, I *can* endure.

When that chapter ended, still unsure of where music would take me next, I found work at Federated Stereo on La Brea and Sunset Boulevards. It felt more familiar. I knew sound. I knew systems. I knew what music *could* be when it was heard the right way. And in that environment, I enjoyed myself. I liked interacting with people. Showing customers something new. Talking specs, demonstrating tone. That was in my wheelhouse. But every day I walked in that store, there was still a part of me wondering, is this it? Am I doing this for the rest of my life? Is Earth, Wind & Fire over for me?

Sometimes the questions were whispered—quiet, insistent fears. And sometimes they were silent, like shadows at the edge of my confidence.

And there was another tension: Customers—friends of music—would come in and see me working the floor. And they'd say things like: "Aren't you in Earth, Wind & Fire?"

And I'd smile, nod, and help them find the perfect speaker setup. But inside . . . it was awkward. It felt like a secret I wasn't sure how to explain. Was I *surviving*? Or was I *waiting*? About six months into the job—I was waiting on a customer—when I saw a familiar figure step through the door.

It took a second to register. There she was—Marilyn White, Maurice's wife, looking for a keyboard for her son, Kahbran.

In that moment, I had a choice.

I could duck into the warehouse and pretend I was stacking boxes until she left—preserve my pride, protect my dignity—or I could meet her with confidence.

For a brief second, I wrestled with myself. But then I walked out onto that floor and said simply, "Marilyn, how can I help you?" She blinked. Quizzically. Recognition spreading slowly across her face.

"Ralph?" She really looked puzzled to see me in a navy-blue polo shirt with a name badge. "What are you doing here?"

I was honest.

"This is where I am . . . until the group figures out what it's going to do."

We didn't sit down for a deep heart-to-heart. Just a few words, a small interaction. I showed her the keyboard she came for. She bought it. She left.

Simple as that.

But in that moment, I wondered if she went home and told Maurice about seeing me in that store—not on stage, not in a spotlight, but just a man working his way through a season.

It was October 1987—the same year Earth, Wind & Fire released a new album, *Touch the World*, featuring the single hit "System of Survival." And if that wasn't enough of a shock . . . I heard it in the store. I heard that song playing—a brand-new Earth, Wind & Fire track—while I was selling stereos in a retail aisle.

That hit me harder than any beat I'd ever played.

Because I was a member of the band pretty much from the beginning. And *no one told me anything* about the album. No heads-up. No call. No conversation. Nothing.

The group had moved on and made a record without me.

At that moment, I stood in that store—surrounded by speakers and soundboards—and felt something deep and sharp inside.

Hurt. Shock. Abandonment.

It felt like being stabbed in the heart. I tried to keep my face calm, but inside . . . I was bleeding. Not physically. Emotionally. Spiritually. I stood there—in that uniform, the corporate name badge pinned to my chest—feeling more stripped down than ever before. Not on a stage. Not in front of thousands. Just in a stereo store, selling sound to strangers.

I was afraid that my hurt, pain, and shock would show on my face. Our song "On Your Face" echoed my sentiments: "Ain't it funny that the way you feel shows on your face? / And no matter how you try to hide, it states your case / Now a frown will bring your spirits down to the ground / And never let you see good things all around / Every time we seem to let our feelings flow / Our luck runs out, and the wind won't blow."

Life doesn't stop just because your dreams get paused. Life doesn't wait for the band to pick up where it left off. Life keeps moving.

The hurt was real. The sense of betrayal was real. The feeling that I had been abandoned by those I had called *brothers* was real. But standing there in that moment I realized something deeper: Pain is not the end of your story. It's the moment you begin to *rewrite* it.

I couldn't have known then how that experience would shape what came next—the resilience it demanded, the humility it carved into me, and the clarity it ultimately gave. When I look back now, years later, with the gift of perspective, that moment in the stereo store wasn't a fall from grace. It was a pivot point where a drummer learned something profound—that life, like music, has its rests and its notes, its unexpected solos and its long pauses. It's the way you *come back* from each challenge that defines your rhythm.

I was sitting at home, just letting the quiet of the evening settle—when the phone rang. On the other end was Art Macnow, our business manager. Calm, steady, and always reliable, he said words I hadn't expected:

"They're putting the original group back together. Do you want to return?"

A miraculous redemption.

That's the closest way I can describe the feeling in my chest when those words hung in the air between us—light and heavy at the same time. It was like being handed a chance to step back into a chapter you never thought you'd revisit, a moment that felt more *restoration* than *reunion*.

If you remember the timeline, the *Touch the World* album—which came out earlier in the decade—was the only one I *didn't* participate in. That gap wasn't by choice. It was by circumstance. But here I was: invited back, welcomed home.

And when I returned to the group, it felt natural—like falling back into a groove I had forgotten was missing from my life. I felt the familiar pulse of the rhythm section, heard the blend of voices, and it came back to me like breath.

But the truth is, the hiatus—and the way it happened—had taken its toll. It wasn't just a break in our touring schedule. It was a break in our trust. A break in rhythm. A break in emotional continuity that wasn't easily stitched back together.

Earlier in the decade, after that pivotal meeting with Maurice—the one that changed so many things—Larry Dunn walked away from the group. Not because he stopped loving the music, but because *how* the pause came down struck him deeply. It affected him more than anyone else because, in his heart, he couldn't believe Maurice would step away from the group in the way he did. Larry was hurt. Confused. Disappointed.

We all believed, at the time, that we would get back on our feet. We believed Maurice's vision would pull us through. But Larry's trust had been shaken, and for him, that rupture lasted longer and deeper than it did for most of us.

And then there was Al McKay—gone off to do his own thing. Creative seeds planted elsewhere. Life shifted in new directions.

The decision to effectively *pause* Earth, Wind & Fire for six long years left a ripple through all of our lives. Not just in our careers—but in our sense of identity. The 1980s became, for me personally, a decade of discomfort. Of longing. Of trying to find meaning outside of something that had once defined me, energized me, and given me purpose.

I won't sugarcoat it—the 1980s were not my favorite decade.

Reflections at the time were heavy, and hindsight only confirms it. There were successes, yes—individual explorations, personal growth—but losing momentum in the band felt like losing part of myself. Earth, Wind & Fire had been more than a career. It was a family, a calling, a rhythm in my blood.

So when Art's call came in 1988, it wasn't just a professional invitation. It was a chance to heal something that had been incomplete for too long. And I said "yes."

As I stepped back into rehearsals and felt those grooves start clicking again—old patterns, new interpretations, familiar laughter in the studio—I felt a sense of homecoming. It was beautiful. Almost effortless at times. The music interlocked like we'd never been apart.

But the emotional residue of the hiatus was still there, like a shadow that didn't quite go away. We all carried it differently. Larry, as I mentioned, found it too hard to reconcile. Al had moved on to pursue his own thing. Others found new chapters in solo work, composing, family life.

And yet, here we were—back together.

I was truly grateful. Grateful that the difficult period had ended. Grateful that the door hadn't been closed forever. Grateful for the chance to honor our history *and* create again.

Something important to understand—our hiatus never went *public* in the sense that people thought we had broken up. We never issued a press release that said, "Earth, Wind & Fire has disbanded."

We were simply on a very long break.

That gap taught me more about who I am than I care to admit. Away from the band, I looked in the mirror and asked myself, "Who am I without the sound? Who am I without the applause? What is *my* identity when the name on the marquee isn't mine?"

Those aren't easy questions. But they're vital because growth often comes through the spaces where we feel lost.

When I stepped back into the fold in 1988, I didn't return as a drummer returning to the kit, but as a man changed by time, reflection, loss, and a deeper sense of purpose. That gap—painful and confusing as it was—gave me a perspective I never would have had otherwise.

I saw how fragile trust can be. I saw how deeply we all loved what we built. I saw the bond between bandmates not just as musical synergy, but as a *family connection.*

The music didn't suffer. In fact, it was stronger because each of us had lived life a little bit more fully. We came back with stories, with perspective, with new soul inside our sound.

And that is part of what Earth, Wind & Fire has always been about—not just *sound*, not just success, but story.

We write it in melody. We live it in life. And we carry it forward in every beat we play.

That's why the comeback in 1988 wasn't just a return. It was a renewal. A reaffirmation. And a reminder that even when the music stops—the *spirit* never does.

During that extended break—the kind no one plans for, but everyone eventually faces—I learned something that no tour, award, or encore could teach me. I learned what I would truly do to care for my family.

See, when you're in Earth, Wind & Fire, the world comes at you with glitter. People see the lights, the costumes, the charts, the sold-out arenas. And don't get me wrong—I've been blessed to stand in that spotlight, night after night, for decades.

But when the lights went dark—when the world slowed, and the crowds stopped singing, and the business paused—I was left with something far more revealing: stillness.

And in that stillness, *truth has a way of stepping forward.* I had to ask myself: Without the stage, the rhythm, the reputation—*who am I?*

And more than that—what *really* matters when all the noise is gone?

I realized in that silence, in that uncertain season, that pride doesn't take care of your family. Ego doesn't hold your hand at night. Accomplishments don't listen to your fears, or fold laundry, or hold things together when the phone stops ringing.

But you know who does?

Susie.

My wife stood by me without flinching. She didn't ask for explanations. She didn't keep score. She didn't expect me to carry the image of "Ralph Johnson the entertainer" when "Ralph Johnson the man" was just trying to breathe through each day.

She simply stayed.

And that kind of loyalty, that kind of *soul-deep patience,* is rare.

Susie confirmed something we both always knew deep down but never had to say out loud until then: *She didn't marry Earth, Wind & Fire.*

She married me.

Not the name in the liner notes. Not the guy in the tailored stage jacket. Me—the quiet, serious one. The introspective one. The flawed one. The man who sometimes overthinks, who needs space to process, who doesn't always have the words but always has the *intent.*

She married *that* man. For better or for worse.

And I saw how Susie never changed. She was steady. Not performative. Not dramatic. Just solid. Like she always had been. She kept the rhythm at home while I figured out how to keep the rhythm inside me.

You really find out who your true supporters are when life throws its worst at you. When things go sideways. When your name doesn't open doors. When your phone's quiet for days at a time. When you're not "on"—you're just *there.*

It's in *those* moments that you find out who sees you for who you really are.

Susie did. And still does.

And more than just seeing me—she reminded me of who I was meant to be.

She never tried to fix it. She never pushed. She just made space—for me to feel, to grieve, to wrestle, to reset. She made sure there was love in the room, even when I couldn't quite reach for it. That kind of support? That's not ordinary. That's a gift.

And during that quiet season, I learned to let go of some things I'd carried for too long—expectations, pressure, that sense of having to be "on" all the time.

Because when you're still for long enough, you start to hear your own soul again.

And one of the first things it whispered to me was this: Tomorrow is promised to no one. Not to me. Not to the band. Not to anyone.

The only guarantee we get is *this day.* This moment. The breath we're taking right now. Everything else? We adjust as it comes.

Life unfolds daily and I must be ready to deal with it. To stay loose in my stance. Flexible in my mind. Open in my heart. Because I never know what's around the corner.

And the truth is, some corners hurt. Some come with silence, or sorrow, or uncertainty. But some? Some open up into miracles. Into new beginnings. Into revelations you couldn't have dreamed up if you tried. That season taught me to stay flexible. Not just physically—which I still work at every morning—but spiritually. Emotionally. I learned how to make peace with not knowing. How to breathe when the map disappears. How to trust the rhythm of *becoming* instead of clinging to the rhythm of *control.*

So now, when people ask me how I made it through that chapter, I tell them the truth:

I had faith. I had discipline. But most of all, I had Susie.

She's not the one who gets interviewed. She's not the one whose name lights up marquees. But her fingerprints are *everywhere* in the story of my survival, my resilience, and my rediscovery.

That's what a real partner is. Not someone who waits for the good times, but someone who *builds with you* during the storms and says, "We're not done yet," even when you're too tired to believe it.

That spotlight might fade, and the tour might pause, but *real love*—that steady, honest, no-flinch kind of love—that's what holds you up when the music stops.

And in its absence, we had to re-learn how to just *be*. How to *listen*. How to get through days not marked by applause or booking sheets, but by little things—grocery lists, home repairs, check-ins with the kids.

But you'll never find them unless you're *willing to stay open*.

I did stay open, and my miracle occurred. The group got back together as Earth, Wind & Fire, but my openness was pushed to another level. I had to forgive to return in the right spirit and mind. I had to forgive Maurice, not so much for his decision to pause the group, but for how he did it. Once I could forgive, I could move forward, and in doing so, we didn't seem to miss a beat musically. There were no more meetings, no more talk about the hiatus. I had to come back with a clean slate, and I couldn't drag any old baggage into what a new beginning was now. There likely were deeper conversations with Phil and Reece, but not with me and the others. We just jumped in and did the thing.

But we played in empty arenas on that *Touch the World* tour, a real reminder that we couldn't pick up right where we left off after a long six-year hiatus. Things were different. Was the love gone? Would we ever recapture the hearts of our fans? If so, it would happen through a song.

There are songs that make you *dance*. There are songs that make you *feel*. And then . . . there are songs that make you *understand yourself in the mirror of someone else's heart.* "After the Love Has Gone" is one of those songs.

It wasn't written in our rehearsal room. It wasn't cooked up on the tour bus. It didn't come from the fire of Maurice's soul in the same way as "Shining Star" or "That's the Way of the World." No—this song came through a circle of great musicians who weren't even in our band at first. And when it landed in our hands, we felt its weight like a heartbeat that wouldn't quit.

I can still remember the first time I heard the demo that David Foster brought to Maurice. David was this young keyboard player and songwriter—already sharp, already polished—working with folks on the West Coast, part of this whole movement of writers who were blurring the lines between pop, soul, and sophisticated adult contemporary. One day, in the middle of an idea, he forgot the words to a song he was working on, and in that moment of forgetfulness, he *made up* a chorus that went, "Oh, ohhh . . . after the love has gone." It was one of those moments where something unexpected lands like a lightning strike.

David and Jay Graydon had already been tossing ideas back and forth, and then they called in Bill Champlin to finish the lyrics. But here's the twist: That song was initially meant to be part of Bill's own record. It wasn't written for us. A lot of people don't know that. It wasn't pitched to a soul group. But when David brought the demo to Maurice White—to us—Maurice was like a kid in a candy store. He heard the emotion in that chorus. He heard the story. And more than anything, he felt *us*—Earth, Wind & Fire—in the melody and the chord changes. Maurice didn't just want to record it—he wanted to interpret it. And when Maurice wants something, that's it. It's on.

We were in the studio working on what would become the *I Am* album in 1978. The record itself was ambitious—strings, horns, soul, funk, pop, and ballads. Most of the stuff was our own writing, but this song . . . This song felt like destiny. Maurice said something once that stayed with me: "*A song doesn't have to come from you to belong with you.*" And that's exactly what "After the Love Has Gone" became.

The band first cut the track in Hollywood. But let me tell you—there was nothing easy about recording it. Verdine told me later that the group tried it six or seven times before Maurice said, "No—it doesn't feel right yet." He could hear the heart of the song, but he wanted the *feel* to match the *feeling.* And you know Maurice—he wasn't going to settle until it was perfect. And when it finally came together? Oh man . . . it lifted. It wasn't just music. It was confession.

Maurice with his grounded warmth and the combination of both him and Phil on background vocals brings about a very memorable performance, and underneath that, the band carried this lush groove. Larry's keys, Verdine's bass, the horns arranged behind the vocals like a heartbeat—all of it was saying something nobody else could say quite the same way.

When we first released it as a single from *I Am* in July 1979, we had no idea it'd become the powerhouse ballad it turned into. But it did—and fast. It climbed to No. 2 on both the Billboard Hot 100 and the R&B charts.

By the time we took it on the road, the audience already knew the song—not just the words, but the *weight* of it. And that's a rare thing. Most ballads are gentle. They ease you in, they lull you, they float. But "After the Love Has Gone"? That's a *story.* It gets into your chest first, then moves up to your throat, and finally settles behind your eyes. It's about *something lost*—love that was real, honest, and full—turned into a memory that *hurts to remember.* That's not a light subject, but the song had this beautiful way of letting folks feel it without drowning in it.

I'll never forget the first time we played it live on a big tour after its release.

We were in Chicago—cold night, but the place was packed like summer. I walked out on stage behind the band, kit set up under the lights, ready for the high-octane funk numbers that opened the evening. But when we signaled to transition into "After the Love Has Gone," the energy in the room changed—like someone dimmed the lights but didn't turn them off.

Maurice stepped to the mic. Barely moved. Just *held* it. Eyes closed. And then that opening line came out, warm and vulnerable:

"For a while, to love was all we could do . . ."

Now, something strange happens in that moment. It's like the collective breath of an audience all releases at once. You can almost feel it physically—a shift in the air. And when Philip came in with those harmonies—oh man—the crowd just melted into the song with us.

Live, this tune had a life of its own. It wasn't about theatrics. It wasn't about flashy solos or extended jams. It was about *connection.* You look out into the audience and see people holding hands, eyes glistening, some out and proud with emotions they weren't ready to carry before that moment.

Playing it night after night, watching grown men close their eyes, watching couples lean into each other—it was humbling. Music like this doesn't just entertain—it *releases* people. We weren't trying to make everyone cry. We were trying to make them *feel.* And they did.

I remember one night in Detroit—sold out, rowdy, ready for a party. But that song . . . it stopped the party. Not in a bad way—it just *shifted* the room's focus inward. You could hear a pin drop. Then, when Maurice hit that high line at the end and the horns came in—man—the applause wasn't just loud—it was *relieved.* Like people were clapping for having *permission* to feel something deep.

It's funny, because most songs about love lost are sung by the person who *lost* it. But our version—with Maurice's grounded delivery and Philip's pure falsetto harmonies—turned it into something bigger. It was love lost *for everyone who ever lost love.* It felt universal.

And you know what's wild? We never thought of it as a "sad" song. To us, it was always about *honesty.* Stripping love down to its durability—or lack thereof—and admitting that while it may *end,* the experience stays with you.

That honesty is what David Foster originally stumbled into when he forgot the words and improvised that unforgettable chorus. That spontaneous moment—the one that wasn't planned—ended up being the *heart* of the song. There were nights where the applause after we played "After the Love Has Gone" felt like a release valve. Like the entire room had been holding tension it didn't even realize was there. And when the song ended, everyone exhaled. Together.

One time in Paris, I was watching from behind the drummer's riser, and in the front row was this couple—young, maybe early twenties—just hugging each other through the whole thing. Neither of them said a word after the song. They just stood there, holding on to that moment. That's power.

Not every song gets that kind of reaction. Not every composition crosses the line between *performance* and *experience*. But this one did. And I think that's why it's still meaningful decades later—not just to us as musicians, but to the people who carry it with them like a secret.

People think ballads like this are simple. Slow. Easy. But here's the truth: They're the hardest songs to *get right*. You can't hide behind a groove. You can't distract with a beat. It's all *exposure*. And when you feel exposed—that's when real connection happens.

When I sit back now and hear the song play—whether it's on the radio, in a movie, or live—I don't just hear the notes. I hear the *story*. I hear the way it changed *us* as a band. I hear how a song that didn't even start as ours became one of our most enduring emotional touchstones.

And most of all—I hear how David Foster's off-the-cuff idea became something that millions could relate to, feel in their hearts, and carry with them.

Music like that? It doesn't go away. It *stays*. Even long after the love is gone.

Chapter 5

THAT'S LIFE

Once Ralph Johnson gets interested in something, he doesn't let it go until he masters it to his satisfaction. Back in the early 1990s, it was the computer thing. People don't know this, but Earth, Wind & Fire would not have a website today if it weren't for Ralph. He taught himself to write code, and he created the first Earth, Wind & Fire website at earthwindandfire.com. He wrote all the text that shared Earth, Wind & Fire history, and he created the artwork.

—Richie Salvato, Earth, Wind & Fire studio manager

When we returned following our six-year layoff, we found out quickly how much the music world had changed around us. Although we were still at CBS Records, the label had a new president, Walter Yetnikoff. During our absence, CBS hadn't been marketing our music effectively, mainly because EWF was producing no new music for them to market. When we hit the stage on our 1988 tour, we expected to play to sold-out venues, but the places we played were at best half-filled. From my place on the stage, I could see many empty seats. Even though our sound hadn't changed, and we had a certified gold album in *Touch the World* that reached No. 3 on the Billboard Top R&B albums, it was a mistake to think we could have stayed away from our audience so long and then expect them to receive us just as they had before. Suddenly, we were no longer riding high with megahit after megahit.

Although fans weren't filling our shows as they had just a few years earlier, we still had the magic for producing hits. We were still writing great songs, and Maurice could still pick hits for the group. To be a hit, though, a song or an album needs two features working for it: the music and studio production and marketing. Earth, Wind & Fire learned that we could have a great song, a great album, but if that music wasn't being marketed well, then we had what I call a "living room" hit. The music's played in your living room, but no one else hears it.

I learned from these moments that timing is everything in music and in life. There's a window of opportunity where everything clicks, and you can do no wrong. But that window won't stay open forever. Trends change, tastes change, and you're yesterday's news before you know it. That's why, when you're in that sweet spot you've got to make the most of it. Keep pushing yourself, keep innovating, and keep building on your successes. Stay focused because there's always someone waiting to take your place.

While we were on CBS/Columbia, Earth, Wind & Fire enjoyed the advantage of working with the president of the label, Clive Davis, who had an ear for creative songwriting and who recognized a great song and a great artist. He had discovered or had nurtured artists like Aretha Franklin, Janis Joplin, Whitney Houston, Alicia Keys, and Barry Manilow. He had the funding to market his artists, and he conveyed to listeners that each artist's voice he supported was the one worthy of listeners' attention. Nobody invested in us like CBS/Columbia, nor was there a president who bravely invested in, believed in, and supported us like Clive Davis.

Since we were a Black R&B band that had crossed over, our appeal was to everyone. We were the right group at the right time at the right record company with the right label president. We didn't try to do that. It just happened with our catchy, uplifting message-oriented music and consistent marketing. We were not just another "Ooh, baby, baby" singing group; we were Earth, Wind & Fire.

In 1993 we rejoined the Warner Bros. label for our sixteenth studio album, the No. 8 R&B Top 100 album *Millennium*, which featured the single "Sunday Morning." EWF had released its first two albums—its self-titled debut album and *The Need of Love*—with Warner Bros. in 1971. I didn't come on board until after those first two Warner Bros. albums and then Clive moved us to CBS/Columbia Records with him. In 1996, we released *Avatar* on the independent label Pyramid, while one year later, in 1997, we released *In the Name of Love* on Rhino Records. In 2003, we released *The Promise* on Kalimba Records. These albums did not reach the same commercial level as our past works, not because the quality of the songs had diminished, but because we weren't receiving the same level of marketing support for those albums as we had for our earlier albums. Many of us in *Earth, Wind & Fire* were frustrated because our creative process had remained the same, our song-making formula was unchanged, and so we should have been booming forever. There was some level of frustration in the group because, in our minds, the high level of success should not have ended.

Still these labels looked for creative ways to market us and broaden our international exposure by releasing a series of greatest hits and live albums: *Gratitude* (1975); *Live in Japan* (1990); *Earth, Wind & Fire Live Tokyo, Japan* (1994); *That's the Way of the World: Alive in '75* (2002); and *Live in Rio* (2002). Live albums were popular and were highly successful in reintroducing EWF to a global audience. *Gratitude* was the most successful, as it had studio cuts and live songs such as "Sing a Song," "Can't Hide Love," and "Devotion." By the time we released that album, with that classic white cover, we had enough material in our catalog to do a great live album.

For our shows, Maurice would develop a setlist that included "Sun Goddess," with Ramsey Lewis, live material from the *That's the Way of the World* album, "Shining Star," "Yearnin' Learnin'," and an extended version of "Reasons," sung by Philip Bailey with a memorable alto sax solo by Don Myrick of the Phenix Horns. There was virtually no difference in performing for international audiences and performing for US fans. Our global brothers and sisters sang along and knew the song lyrics even though they could not speak English. The Japanese were our most loyal fans and were not concerned about our having new hits. I'll never forget the last time we did Japan with Maurice was in 1996. They sang along to every song, and we left reinvigorated and inspired.

In addition to the changes Earth, Wind & Fire faced with marketing and audiences, we were transforming ourselves as a group. When we resumed in 1988, the drummer and brother of Maurice, Fred White, didn't return. Sonny Emory replaced him. Guitarist Al McKay had gone, and the talented Sheldon Reynolds came on board. Larry Dunn didn't continue on the keyboards, and Vance Taylor filled his post. These were significant personnel changes, but it didn't take them any time to fall into the Earth, Wind & Fire groove; all of these new musicians breathed fresh life into our music. They had grown up with our sound and didn't miss a beat as they stepped in to keep the group flying at its highest level.

One of the most positive personnel changes was Sonny Emory. Sonny was a great drummer who even inspired a longtime veteran like myself. While we would do an occasional drum thing, I never returned to drums full-time but became a vocalist up front. Sheldon, too, was a great addition as a fine guitarist and solid vocalist who covered many of Maurice's solos when he could no longer tour with us by 1994.

Transitions also gave way to opportunities for growth. Maurice was no longer touring with us, but he was still recording. He had his voice, but I could begin to hear that he didn't have the same vocal strength he once had. I was finally able to write some songs with him. We wrote a tune titled "Welcome" on the *Heritage* album, released in 1990. That was a special moment for me because he could see another side of my musical talent and encouraged me to continue to be a more active writer in the group.

On that same album, the legendary Sly Stone came in to co-write with Robert Brookins and sing the song "Good Time" with Maurice. They would go into the studio by themselves, just as Maurice and Philip would do. It wasn't like all of us were there to observe. They worked on their vocals separately. I wasn't there when those vocals would be done. It was a whole separate scene, and I was there for tracking and percussion. Those vocal sessions were usually Maurice and Phil, or whoever the principal vocalists were, and George Massenburg, who was a brilliant engineer—not just a recording engineer, but an electrical engineer as well. He had a little lab at the Complex where he could record and play with sound, tinker with things. The George Massenburg Labs, they're still using his EQs today.

My moving from a primarily instrumentalist role to being a vocalist up front happened in the most unusual way. George Faison of *The Wiz* fame directed us when we were filming *Sgt. Pepper's Lonely Hearts Club Band.* We were setting up the shot for the song "Got to Get You into My Life," our remake of the Beatles classic. Phil and Maurice were out front, and George looked at the shot and, out of nowhere, said, "Hey Ralph. Get off the drums. Come up here, grab a mic, and stand right here next to Maurice."

After 1988, I never returned to the drums but was integrated as a vocalist.

You *see* and *feel* the music differently depending on where you're standing—and I've had the rare gift of standing in both places.

Behind the drum kit, tucked back in the pocket of the band, you're in the engine room of the operation. You're not out there dancing with the spotlight—you're down in the machinery, making sure the ship stays on course. When I'm drumming, I'm in a deep mental zone—I'm the one keeping time, maintaining the groove, locking everyone in.

Let me tell you something about drummers: We hear *everything*. Every subtle shift, every hesitation, every flourish from the horns or lift in the lead vocal—it all lands in our ears. That's because we're the heartbeat. You can't zone out, not even for a second. One tiny misstep in tempo, and everything else unravels. The whole band's built on that pulse.

It's a very powerful, yet humble, position to be in.

You're not out front taking the bow . . . but you're driving the whole thing from behind. You learn to lead without being seen.

Now, being up front? It's a whole different world. It's theatrical. It's visceral. It's human to human.

When I stepped away from the drums and moved into my role as a vocalist, I experienced the music—and the moment—in a totally different way. The air changes. The stakes shift. You're not just providing rhythm anymore—you're making eye contact, speaking directly to people, and the feedback is *instant.*

As a singer, I can look someone in the audience dead in the eye and say something as simple as: "What's happening?" or "Hey—I like your tie."

And that might sound small. But when you're on a stage, and the crowd is 3,000 strong—or 20,000—and you connect with one person that way? It's not small.

That's what I've grown to *love* about being up front. I can reach out and touch a moment. I can pull people into the show and let them know, *I see you. I'm here with you. This isn't just performance—this is a shared experience.* It's more exposed. More vulnerable. But it's also more free.

When I'm in front, I'm still *listening*, of course. That never stops. Right now, there are two players I keep especially close ears on: John Paris, our drummer, and Myron McKinley, our keyboardist and musical director.

John is *rock solid* behind the kit. He understands the foundation of our sound. He knows the space between the notes—the breath of the beat—and he honors the legacy of the grooves that Maurice, Fred White, and I laid down across decades. I listen to him the way a pilot listens to his co-pilot—ready, in sync, and trusted.

And Myron? Myron is a *force*. He's one of those rare musicians who not only plays the instrument with mastery—he lives in it. His choices are tasteful, unexpected, and brilliant. I can always tell when he's trying something new, too. He'll shift the color of a chord—just slightly—and my ear picks it up immediately. I'll turn my head, raise an eyebrow, and he'll flash me that smile like, *"Yeah, I knew you'd catch that."*

That's what musicianship is—a conversation within a conversation.

Even though I'm not sitting at the kit anymore during the whole show, I'm *still drumming in my head.* I'm counting time. I'm feeling every downbeat and offbeat. I'm scanning the dynamic waves—high and low—and holding on to the throughline of the setlist like I'm reading sheet music made out of feeling.

People sometimes ask me, "Which do you prefer? Drums or vocals?"

And the truth is, I don't choose between them. They're different *languages*, but they both tell the same story.

Drumming is how I entered the conversation—it's how I earned my place in Earth, Wind & Fire. It's where I learned discipline, endurance, and the invisible leadership it takes to hold a band together from behind.

But being out front as a vocalist . . . that's where I get to speak. That's where I get to smile at someone in the third row or throw a peace sign to the couple dancing in the aisles. That's where I get to breathe with the crowd.

What a gift it is to have had both of these perspectives—to know what it feels like to *build the rhythm from the back* and then to *ride the wave from the front.* I know most people never get to experience both. But I did and still do.

And I wouldn't trade either for anything. Maurice was able to live in both spaces too, so his inability to tour anymore was a pivotal moment for us. Maurice never sat down with us and said, "I have Parkinson's." But we knew. We could see it. I recognized something was wrong as I saw the trembling of his hands. I knew something was going on, but, at first, I didn't know what. Eventually, Maurice couldn't continue. I could hear it in his voice. He didn't have the strength that he had before. The three of us—Philip Bailey, Verdine White, and I—had to decide if we should fold it all up because Maurice could no longer go out. Would our fans accept us and still come to see Earth, Wind & Fire shows that didn't include Maurice? Of course, we were committed to maintaining the EWF sound we had all along. That wasn't a lot of discussion. The main discussion was, *Could we pull off a tour without Maurice?*

Having to give up touring took its toll on Maurice. He couldn't imagine the band being out there without him in it, and we couldn't imagine being without Maurice. Initially, he didn't want to allow the group to go out on its own, but one of our managers, Bob Cavallo, reminded Maurice that in Earth, Wind & Fire he had created a life force and that even though he could no longer contribute to its energy on tour, he should allow it to continue to grow and to carry the energy to its fans. Maurice agreed with Cavallo, and Art Macnow and Richie Salvato oversaw the band's touring activities on Maurice's behalf. Whenever Maurice wanted something done, he would call Richie and say, "Hey Rich, I need . . ."

Rich would agree to look into it and Maurice would always say, "Yeah, see what you can do?"

Maurice preferred for his brother Verdine to lead the group, but Verdine couldn't, or wouldn't, do it. Verdine was already the band leader, anyway, handling all the sound checks and keeping up with everyone in the band. Everyone respected him, but he didn't seem to be able to handle much outside the mundane tasks of leading a band. Either he didn't have the desire or didn't want the added responsibility, but Verdine tried to please everybody and seldom challenged any new ideas. Wanting to avoid drama, he would go along with whatever Philip suggested, often to the frustration of the rest of us. Even Richie in management said to Verdine, "You're the fricking guy that was by Maurice's side building this band from the inception. Tell Phil what you think and take charge."

We eventually enlisted Robert Brookins from Sacramento as a musical director in the mid-to-late '90s. He was very talented and capable, but he started taking the band in a whole different direction. Maurice would say to Rich and the management team in the early days when he gave permission for the band to go out, "You have to watch them for me. Make sure they don't ruin the integrity of the band." So, whenever Rich thought we were going in a different direction, he'd come backstage and say the show was good, but he'd remind Phil, now the band's leader, "You gotta pay attention to this or that."

When we played at Lake Tahoe, Rich finally got Maurice's ear, reminding Maurice, "You know you told me to watch the band." Maurice nodded in agreement. "Why don't I sneak you into a show so you can see what's going on?" Rich suggested. Rich sneaked him into the Tahoe show, and Maurice sat at the sound console.

"See what he's doing onstage," Rich would say.

Maurice would nod, "I get it. He's making it his own."

"Yeah, but did you want it to go that far and have the show go in a completely different direction?" Rich would reply.

Maurice got a little annoyed by the observation, and he went backstage after the show and gave the band a surprise critique. He shared what he thought and would encourage band members along the way. Robert continued his role through our performance at the 2002 Winter Olympics in Salt Lake City, Utah. He was eventually followed by new musical directors Morris Pleasure, and later, Mike McKnight. Rich and the management team continued their work in protecting and advising us until Art Macnow passed away due to complications arising from cancer.

We put on a six-week tour to test the market, performing for the first time in our lives without our founder, lead writer, co-lead singer, mentor, and guide. Of course, with all the personnel changes in the band and with Maurice no longer leading us, we didn't know whether audiences would respond favorably to us. At first, it took some time to find out if we still had the magic. Fans also took a while to get used to Maurice's absence.

New York was cold that night. It wasn't a blizzard or a deep freeze, just one of those clear Manhattan evenings when the wind slices up the avenues like it's late for something. You step outside and every bit of exposed skin tightens. We were playing Radio City Music Hall—not our first time, not our last. But this time was different. It was our first New York show since Maurice had stopped performing live.

Now, I'd stood on thousands of stages by then. Big ones. Tiny ones. Legendary ones. But that night . . . this one felt heavy. Like the air itself was holding its breath.

We were well into the show when "Fantasy" came up on the setlist. I'd known it was coming—of course I did—but still, seeing the word printed on the page just above my monitor gave me a feeling I couldn't quite name. Not dread. Not fear. Just weight. Like someone had laid a velvet cloak across my shoulders, something beautiful, but undeniable.

We had adjusted the arrangement slightly since Maurice no longer performed. Not to replace him—no one could do that—but to make room for the space he left behind. Philip handled the lead vocal, as always. But the intro? That ethereal, glittering lift that opened the door to another world? That was Maurice's soul, and it still hovered there, every time.

Backstage, before the show, there was a photo of Maurice on the green room wall. Black-and-white. Smiling. Calm. He wasn't posing. He wasn't performing. Just Maurice—watching. I remember touching the edge of the frame before I went out. Not for luck. For connection.

Then the intro began. The keys floated in like stardust—delicate, layered, the exact sound of a dream being born. The synth shimmered, that little scale cascading like glass marbles down marble steps. Then came the strings—real ones tonight, a full quartet sitting to our left in the shadows. And just like that . . . we weren't in New York anymore.

That's the power of "Fantasy." From the first note, the world changes shape.

Then Philip stepped forward. He didn't rush. He didn't even walk. He *glided.* One spotlight followed his path across the stage. The crowd went still. No phones in the air. No shouting. Just *attention.*

He opened his mouth—and Maurice was there.

"Every man has a place, in his heart there's a space . . . And the world can't erase his fantasies . . ."

Phil's voice didn't mimic Maurice's. He wasn't impersonating. He was honoring. And I felt it. We all did. You could see it in Verdine's posture—just a hair more still, like he was letting the moment speak before the bass line took its place. You could see it in the horns, who normally danced with bravado, now standing reverently, instruments resting by their sides for that first verse. Me? I was watching the air.

It's hard to explain, but drummers—good ones—learn to read a room's rhythm like a second skin. And that night, the air was pulsing with something . . . otherworldly. Not grief exactly. Not nostalgia. Something deeper. Like presence. Absence turned inside out.

And then it happens. The B section, and now the chorus joins in. "And we will live together."

This is one of the moments in the show when I love singing the background harmonies. Harmonic intention. "Fantasy," one of my favorites.

That's the strange, beautiful thing about "Fantasy." For a song rooted in imagination, it's never been escapism. It's *invitation.* It asks you to step outside your pain, your noise, your routine, and remember the *bigness* of who you are. Of what life could be.

And that night, in that city, without Maurice physically with us? It meant more than it ever had.

As we moved into the bridge, I glanced stage left, where Maurice always used to stand during this part—hand on the mic stand, eyes closed, swaying in that grounded, quiet way of his. The spotlight would hit him, and he'd look like he was pulling energy straight from the cosmos. That space was empty now. But I swear I saw him.

Not literally. Not as a ghost or a silhouette. But in a way that bypassed vision entirely. In the rhythm. In the warmth rising from the stage floor. In the silence of the audience between lines. *He was there.*

And it hit me: He would've *loved* this night. The sound was perfect. The crowd was listening. The musicians were *in it.* No ego. No flash. Just presence. Just music.

Maurice always said: "Don't play the part. *Be* the part." So I did.

Then came the final chorus. We went *big.* Horns cutting sharp angles. Strings rising in harmony. Philip's falsetto floating higher and higher, pushing into a range that felt less like sound and more like emotion in flight. Verdine's bass drove it all like an engine on fire. And me? I hit harder. Not loud. Just *true.* Each crash cymbal hit was a thank-you. Each kick drum pulse, a heartbeat for the man who built us. Each snare hit, a memory.

Then, after a moment that felt like a held breath across the city . . . Applause. Thunderous. Long. Real. The kind that doesn't ask for another song—it says, "Thank you. We felt that." We stood there, letting it wash over us. Not milking it. Just being with it. And I thought: *He's still here.* Not just in the arrangement. Not just in the vocals. But in the way we carry ourselves. In the way we *listen* to one another onstage. In the way we give the music room to shine, not just burn.

Backstage later, someone asked me what it felt like to play "Fantasy" without Maurice. I smiled. "You don't play it *without* him," I thought. "You play it *for* him. And with him. Every time."

That's what "Fantasy" is. It's not an escape. It's a *return*. To who we were. To what we love. To who we miss. To the dream that never dies, even when the dreamer moves on.

Although both the band and the fans missed Maurice, we didn't get discouraged or fold up or cave in. Our fans embraced Earth, Wind & Fire without Maurice because our music transcended all of us, and people wanted to hear it.

This new arrangement worked well, initially. Slowly, though, small cracks in our foundation eventually drove a wedge between members of the group, resulting in changes in the makeup of Earth, Wind & Fire.

In 2003, we released *The Promise*. I think Phil might've been slightly agitated as he felt he should've been more involved with the creative process, and I can dig it!

Maurice had asked Ron Ellison, his good friend and a promo man from Warner Bros. whose relationship with Maurice went back quite a few years, to pitch this next album to the group. Maurice trusted him. While Rich of our management team thought this would be a hard sell, Ron said he would go in and tell the group what he thought. Ron thought the group would buy the pitch because "they're old guys and will do what they are told." Although Rich emphatically warned Ron that he needed to present a coherent plan to the group, Ron ignored that advice, showing us no respect and presenting his half-baked idea for the album. Our faces spoke volumes as we non-verbally hung him out to dry.

Two days later, Barry White's manager Ned Shankman came in and did a proper pitch. He had a bullet point presentation, a book with all these pictures, and talked about how he would make us a lot of money and increase our worth. It was impressive.

Following this pitch meeting with Ned Shankman, Maurice agreed with the group and Rich that we'd hire Shankman to lead the efforts on this new album, *Illumination*. With Shankman's vision, EWF believed we could make a new album that sounded like EWF, reflected our evolution as a group, and our commitment to deliver transcendent music to our fans. I wasn't highly attracted to the album, maybe except for some of the guest artists like Kelly Rowland, Big Boi, Kenny G, Brian McKnight, will.i.am, and others. Our hopes were short-lived, though, for Ron went directly to Maurice and complained; whatever Ron said caused Maurice to change his mind again and to choose Ron over Ned.

When Phil discovered Maurice's betrayal, he was upset and said, "Forget this album project altogether." We decided that we were not going to support this album, and we were not going to talk about it on the road. Phil told us: "I have a guy with whom I was going to do a personal project. But I won't do it. I'll give my concept to EWF." Phil was adamant about having a whole new, fresh look. He brought in Damien

Smith as the manager for *Illumination*, our nineteenth album, which we released in 2005. The discussion moved to lawyers Henry Root and Richard Lair, who worked out the licensing deal. It was a tense moment for all of us.

Sometime after our twentieth studio album, *Now Then & Forever*, was released in 2013 with the single "I Promise," Damien and EWF eventually parted ways after the Kennedy Center Honors in 2019. Suddenly, we didn't hire that next-level manager we desperately needed who would look out for us and help us plan our next move.

Even though our most diehard fans knew about our transitions, they continued to support us because our sound remained unchanged. Our story might have turned out differently if all these management and personnel changes had resulted in a radically new sound. But the music we were making retained its special EWF vibe and quality. Even now, our sound is recognizable, and we play as hard as ever to take our fans on a musical journey. Philip's falsetto is vibrant as ever, Verdine's energy on the bass is still blasting, and I'm consistently holding down percussion and adding to vocals. We three will always be the core of Earth, Wind & Fire. No one will ever fire us or push us out of the group. Verdine, Phil, and I keep pushing the group to the next level, as well as maintaining our heritage.

Even though we were not releasing hit after hit any longer, we were still popular, and we were doing what Maurice had always intended: to reach fans with our music and to give them great quality music with a great message. That's what mattered most to us. We didn't make records to win Grammys. However, we worked hard and committed ourselves to our vision and our music, and we received those industry accolades because we did the work.

I believe musicians today are working their hardest to produce great music, not just to win awards. If one is a true artist, it's about doing quality work, not about winning accolades and awards. Whether we played the large 20,000-seat arenas like the Capital Centre in DC or the humongous European outdoor arena music festivals down to the smallest venues like the Uptown Theatre in Philly that seated about 1,000 or any venue size in between, we played to elevate our audiences to a happier, more positive mental state, to make their world a better place for at least a few hours.

I learned from all these events that you can spend your life perfecting your craft, your image, and brand, and when something unexpected happens, people will desert you. But the whole of your work is greater than one altered part. People feel and respond to authenticity. I saw the resilience of our well-established brand and the loyalty of our fan base remain intact because we did. Being true to who you are allows the essence of what makes you special and gives you the strength to endure.

That disappointing *Touch the World* tour brought home a reality. When you are used to 20,000 people enthusiastically screaming and hollering at every song, and that height is diminished six years later, you question your future. Like Frank Sinatra once sang, "You're riding high in April, shot down in May / But I know I'm gonna change that tune / When I'm back on top in June." I was not so concerned that I would bail like some bandmates. I believed I needed to continue riding this dream until June arrived. And it would.

Chapter 6

In Pursuit of the Spirit Within

Dad would always say, "To whom much is given, much is required." He lives by that. He tries to be giving and does that well. Maybe that is part of the reason why Earth, Wind & Fire is still going on. They're generous in giving love through their music. They speak to a particular need we all have as human beings . . . EWF provides people a musical blueprint for how to live and how to be in touch with that warm place in the universe.

—Mark-Anthony Johnson, youngest son,
community organizer

You never know when you will speak your last words. The world's light dimmed in 2016 when Maurice White, due to Parkinson's complications, said his last words at age 74. It was the end of an era. The only album we recorded without

Maurice—*Now Then & Forever*—was released in 2013, featuring the single "I Promise."

Maurice's passing caught me unprepared. We had just done this interview about the Grammy Lifetime Achievement Award. Not long after, our manager at that time, Damien Smith, called and said, "Ralph, I have some news for you. Maurice just passed." Shocked, I said, "Whaaat!" It was like getting hit in the head with a sledgehammer.

Even now, years later, it sits in my chest like something unfinished—something that can't quite be spoken into shape. You don't get over a loss like that. You carry it. Quietly. Respectfully. Like a sacred weight.

I remember his private memorial service in Ladera Heights, Los Angeles. It was intentionally small, intentionally restrained. Maurice would have wanted it that way. He was never one for grand public displays. Privacy mattered to him. Stillness mattered.

And yet—despite the limits on attendance—*everybody* was there.

Everybody who mattered. Everybody who knew. Everybody who had felt his influence, even if they'd only crossed paths once. There were remembrances of Maurice's Memphis roots, his moving to Chicago to study music at the Chicago Conservatory of Music where he honed his drumming skills. Some reminisced about his being a staff drummer at Chess Records, playing for legends like Etta James and Muddy Waters.

The room carried a hush that wasn't empty—it was heavy with recognition. You looked around and saw faces from every corner of music and culture. The Wu-Tang Clan was there, heads bowed. Cedric the Entertainer, Margaret Cho—all grieving, all quiet. And those who couldn't be there physically still made themselves present: Prince, Alicia Keys, Bruno Mars—sending official tributes, flowers, messages of love and respect.

Stevie Wonder was there. Pharrell Williams. Dionne Warwick. Former managers. Fellow musicians. Industry people who had seen it from the inside and understood exactly what had been lost.

Some flew in from across the country just to be in that place. Morris Pleasure came in from Atlanta. Drummer Sonny Emory was there. Harvey Mason—I remember seeing him and pulling him into a long embrace. No words. Just a hug that said everything.

The Waters—those legendary background singers—were there. Quiet, reverent, standing in the space Maurice helped make possible.

Ramsey Lewis was there. Early in his career, Maurice had joined his trio, won a Grammy with Ramsey, and discovered the kalimba—the African thumb piano that would become a signature sound for Earth, Wind & Fire. Ramsey got up and told a story that brought both laughter and ache. He talked about the day Maurice came to him and said, *"I'm starting a band."* Ramsey said he laughed, not really taking him seriously, and told Maurice to *"take an aspirin and go back to sleep."*

The room smiled. Because here we were. Maurice left Ramsey in 1969, formed his own group, The Salty Peppers, which evolved into Earth, Wind & Fire. Apparently, Maurice had been very serious.

Ramsey played the piano and spoke with warmth, humility, and respect. Bob Cavallo, one of our former managers, said a few words—measured, heartfelt, grounded in history. Stevie Wonder spoke, too. He didn't perform, but his words carried the weight of love and deep understanding. When Stevie speaks about another artist, you listen differently.

It was a tough service for me. I don't remember every word that was said, but I remember how it felt.

I sat there surrounded by people—rows and rows of them—but internally, I was alone. Silent. Rewinding the tape of my life with Maurice. Replaying moments only the two of us shared. Conversations. Rehearsals. Quiet car rides. Decisions made in passing that ended up shaping decades.

My friend Kenny Dickerson at one point said later, *"Man, Ralph looked devastated."*

He was right. I was. It was written all over my face. In my eyes. In the way my shoulders slumped forward instead of standing tall. I wasn't trying to hide it. I didn't have the energy to. Grief doesn't ask permission. What hurt the most wasn't just losing a bandleader or a visionary. I had lost a friend. A fellow drummer. A man who had quietly shaped the course of my life.

As I sat there, my mind drifted to the subtleties of Maurice's creativity—the things people didn't always see.

Maurice carried a coloring book and colored pencils with him. Not as a joke. Not as nostalgia. As a practice.

I remember flipping through that coloring book once and being completely stunned. His sense of color—how he blended, how he layered, how he balanced contrast and harmony—it was *brilliant.*

And suddenly it all made sense. The album covers. The stage designs. The symbolism. The way Earth, Wind & Fire always looked as intentional as it sounded. That wasn't random.

That was Maurice. He didn't just *hear* music. He saw it.

Losing him meant losing the man who painted the picture before the rest of us even knew what canvas we were standing on.

That service was introspective. Not dramatic. Not loud. It was a mirror—forcing me to look back on everything we'd built together. The risks Maurice took. The confidence he carried. The way he held us all to a higher standard without ever raising his voice.

He had a vision for this group—*and he executed it.* Not halfway. Not cautiously, but in a grand way.

And there I was, sitting in silence, realizing that an era had truly ended. The architect was gone. But the structure he built? It was still standing.

And as painful as that day was—as heavy as it remains—I also felt something else, quietly forming beneath the grief: gratitude. Gratitude that I got to walk beside him. Gratitude that I got to learn from him. Gratitude that I got to be part of something he dreamed into existence.

Some people live entire lives and never meet someone who changes their trajectory. I met Maurice. And even now, in his absence, his presence still guides me. That memorial didn't close a chapter but opened a new one.

As grief-stricken as I was, when it was my time to speak about Maurice, I remember telling a joke because Maurice always loved a great joke. He had this memorable laugh. I told a joke that I once had told Maurice about a burglar who broke into a house and he started up on the second floor and worked his way down. The burglar knew the family was gone on vacation as they did every year. As he was going through the house, ransacking it, he kept hearing a voice that said, "Jesus is watching you."

The burglar finally works his way downstairs and the voice is now louder: "Jesus is watching you."

He's got his flashlight and is looking around; over in the corner, it looks like a birdcage covered up. So, he goes over and pulls off the cover, and sure enough, it's a bird.

The bird says, "Jesus is watching you."

The guy tries to get friendly with the bird and says, "Hey, little birdie, what's your name? The bird says, "Moses."

And the burglar says, "What kind of stupid pet owner would name a bird Moses?"

And the bird replies, "The same owner that would name his Rottweiler 'Jesus.'"

Jokes aside, when I reflect on Maurice's impact on my life, what strikes me most isn't just the music he helped create, but the leadership he embodied—steady, unflinching, and uniquely his own. I didn't just miss his guidance after he passed. No—I missed his *leadership*. The kind that doesn't shout but resonates.

Maurice was a decade older than the rest of us, and that gave him an edge—not in ego, but in perspective. While we were still figuring things out, he *had* things figured out. He knew what he wanted—musically, spiritually, and existentially. And he pursued it with a clarity that was both inspiring and humbling to witness.

To the outside world, Maurice could appear mysterious—almost elusive. He wasn't one to chase attention. He wasn't the life of the party or the guy in the front row of every industry event. That wasn't Maurice. He moved with intention, and he was very careful about where he appeared and why.

You might find that surprising, but it's true: We never attended the Grammy Award shows in any official capacity—even when we were nominated, even when we won. Oh sure, I went once with Al McKay in 1983, but it wasn't because we were slated to win or were recognized that night. We just wanted to *see the Grammys.* It wasn't something Maurice cared to spend his energy on. He didn't want to be part of the spectacle—he wanted to *make the music.*

So often, when Earth, Wind & Fire's name was called at awards ceremonies, you would never see Maurice up on that stage on television accepting the trophy. He stayed true to his values: lead with substance, not with spotlight.

It wasn't until much later—after Maurice had transitioned—that Phil, Dean, and I allowed ourselves to step into that wider world of appearances, engagements, and social visibility. But that era was never Maurice's style. His focus was inward—on the work, on the message, on the journey.

When Maurice was gone, it was tough.

Not just because we lost our founder and bandmate, but because we lost our guide—the person who had a vision for this collective soul of sound we lived in. He was anchored. He didn't waver. He didn't lose his center.

And when he left us, the ground felt unsteady for a minute.

But God wakes you up the next day—and when He does, you still have work to do. For Phil, Verdine, and me, that work didn't stop. It transformed.

Just as naturally as Maurice had taken us from dream to reality, Phil stepped into the leadership role. It wasn't awkward or contested. It wasn't even discussed. It simply *made sense*. It was unanimous—in spirit and in logic. Why? Because Phil was one of the three remaining original members. He was our co-lead singer, a principal writer of many of our hits, and one of the most recognizable voices and personalities of the group. The transition wasn't just practical—it was the right next chapter.

Phil wrote in the liner notes of our last studio album *Now Then & Forever* in 2013, "The spirit of the band has always been about uplifting the consciousness of humanity. There's hope that this Earth, Wind & Fire music will go on forever."

That wasn't just a line. That was a mission statement rooted in Maurice's original vision—elevated, carried forward—and still true.

Because of Maurice White, I firmly believe Earth, Wind & Fire will endure.

And as long as I have breath, *I will commit myself to improving this world—helping one person at a time.*

When someone close to you passes—especially someone like Maurice—it forces you to confront your own mortality. You find yourself asking, *How much longer do I have here? What do I want to leave behind?* Tomorrow hasn't been promised to anyone—not to me, not to you, not to anyone reading this.

That's a humbling thought.

And it inevitably makes you reflect on what you're doing *today*—not what you want to accomplish in some distant future.

One of the core lessons Maurice taught me was the importance of an open mind.

He didn't close himself off to a single way of thinking or believing. He wasn't rigid. He wasn't bound by one interpretation of spirituality or philosophy. Maurice was curious—deeply curious—about *humanity*, the forces that shape us, and the wisdom hidden in diverse traditions.

And he didn't just read music books. He read broadly.

You'd walk into Maurice's house and you'd see shelves lined with books that spanned topics, cultures, and eras: *The Laws of Success* by Napoleon Hill—a book about cultivating mastery and aligning minds for a unified purpose, self-development, and psychological texts that influenced his approach to performance and human behavior, spiritual and philosophical writings from many world traditions

Maurice was studying the human journey.

He wasn't satisfied with a narrow road. He wanted the *panorama*—the full view. He wasn't going to lock himself into one box and call it the only truth.

In fact, Maurice introduced me early in my adult life to books that shaped not just *my craft*, but *my character*—texts like:

- *Psycho-Cybernetics* by Dr. Maxwell Maltz—a deep dive into self-image and the psychology of transformation
- *The Master Key to Riches* and *Think and Grow Rich* by Napoleon Hill—books that taught us about mindset, purpose, and the architecture of success

Maurice didn't just read these books for himself—he *applied* principles from them to Earth, Wind & Fire. One especially influential idea was the concept of the "Mastermind"—an alliance of minds united for a single purpose. Maurice applied that not as a gimmick but as a way of life—we were united, focused, and working toward a shared mission.

He also cared about health, not just spiritually or musically, but physically. He introduced me to dietary principles that have stayed with me all my life—eating nutritiously and avoiding processed foods, understanding that what you put in your body affects what you *can* do with your body.

Maurice also recommended *Eat to Live* by Elijah Muhammad—a book about dietary principles rooted in affordable, nutritious food: whole grains, vegetables, fruits, and the importance of loving your body with intention.

Those lessons weren't fads. They became a lifestyle. And because of Maurice, I adapted them and still benefit from those principles today. I still use organic and herbal remedies for pain. My youngest son Mark-Anthony, who was born January 9, 1984, remembers:

When I was about four years old, I was in the kitchen with my mom, who was about to go to work. My dad was asleep. Mom had just finished cooking breakfast, and we had these coil stoves, the ones that would heat up and get bright red. The stove was still hot, but the coils were black, so I put my hands on it. AHHHH! I hollered in pain. My dad rushed into the room, gently picked me up and took me to the bathroom where he cut a piece of aloe vera plant, fanned it out, and put the aloe vera on my hand. The pain just went away! How did he do that! How did a plant . . . My dad had this whole body of knowledge about how to fix things organically. I don't know where he got it.

I respect the body I live in, and I learned that in my youth with Maurice. My body is not simply an instrument, but a vessel of my life. I still engage in healthy practices. Maybe today, that's why we will have a massage therapist come in after a show or have the best caterers bring us the finest foods to keep our bodies fit.

Maurice's wife, Marilyn, worked at a health food store and helped introduce him—and by extension, all of us—to natural, organic nutrition. I remember asking Maurice once how he maintained such clear skin and radiant energy. He introduced me to soy-derived lecithin—and I've never forgotten it.

Maurice's approach was practical, grounded, and holistic. He wasn't attached to a *single* spiritual doctrine. He believed in higher consciousness, but he didn't preach doctrine.

He simply read, learned, explored, and integrated. That openness influenced more than just his worldview. It influenced us. We were a band of avid readers—and that's not something most people expect when they think of a funk and soul group from the '70s. But that's how we operated.

Philip still reads constantly. When we're on the road, you'll find him with a book or audiobook in hand. Dean is the same—on the plane, tablet open, eyes scanning pages or listening with intent.

Yet even with all this broad reading and curiosity, there was *one spiritual truth* that anchored me personally, my Christian faith. My foundation in monotheism—belief in one God—came from my parents. They raised me in it. Sunday School every week. Vacation Bible School every summer on Hobart Boulevard. Even though Maurice explored many expressions of spirituality, that inner compass of faith was something I carried forward from childhood.

It's easy to grow out of those childhood influences and not consciously think about the training our parents provided, but subconsciously, you don't forget the teachings you were raised with. Proverbs 22:6 contains an enduring truth: "Train up a child in the way he should go, and when he is old, he will not depart from it." There have been times during my fifty-year journey with Earth, Wind & Fire when things happened, and I knew those moments "had to be God." When I was asked to return to the group after the six-year hiatus, that was a God thing.

Maurice didn't reject faith. He *expanded* it. He showed us that the pursuit of wisdom is not exclusive to one book, one tradition, or one language. He believed in *exploration*—of ideas, of people, of the world. That's a legacy I carry with me every day.

A leader isn't just someone who tells you where to go. A leader shows you, not what to think, but how to *think*. A leader opens doors in your heart that you didn't know were unlocked. And Maurice? He opened *many*.

There was a spirituality about the group. We took some heat from some television pastors about the *All 'n All* album because of the spiritual symbols and signs. They wanted to degrade and convolute what we were doing and make us into something we were not. But we passed that, and our real fans didn't criticize us. Our popularity and critical acclaim only grew. Maybe it was because we tried to walk the walk of what we talked. You never saw any glaring headlines about Earth, Wind & Fire involved in some nefarious, corruptive, demoralizing, or degrading activity. Some in the entertainment industry are great at talking the talk but not walking the walk.

Many people think God is a joke. One day we will all stand before God and be judged. That's a jolting thought. And some believe that Jesus Christ is nonexistent because he's no longer walking around here. I can only know the path I'm on. I pray every day. I sit in that room and pray because I need to have a personal connection with God. Some of you might be unsettled with all I am sharing, but consider this: Will you know Ralph Johnson, the person, any better for reading this book? It's more than reading about touring, making hit songs, and being part of a famous group. Like Maurice, when he founded Earth, Wind & Fire, my goal is to lift all of us in humanity with love.

I think the fact that the group, after fifty years, is still one of the most sought-after groups and respected bands ever is a God thing. Some things in life are just God things; you must recognize and respect that. You don't have any control over it and didn't make it happen.

I believe in Christianity and Jesus Christ. He will return. I don't necessarily pray for things that I can do myself. If you're going to pray, pray for something only God can do. I do admit that I prayed for EWF to come back together and go back out and be a group again. He allowed that to happen, and I am eternally grateful.

Some people find their spiritual course when they hit rock bottom. My adult spiritual journey didn't happen when I was sweating it out during my construction gig work. Yes, I prayed for the group to get back together, but even in that difficult time, I knew God was my sustainer. Christ spoke to me, and I accepted him when I was on top.

It was 1976, and we had just released our *Spirit* album ("Imagination," "On Your Face"), our third multiplatinum-selling album in a row. I lived in Hollywood, 2260 Cahuenga Boulevard, Apartment 405, a big apartment building right off the 101 freeway. I woke up one Sunday morning and was moved to act. I called Al McKay and said, "Hey Al, let's go to church."

Surprisingly, he said, "Okay, let's do it." We visited Frederick K. Price's Church, the Crenshaw Christian Center. We attentively listened to the message, and when Pastor Price gave the invitation, we both went up. That day, as an adult,

I gave my life to Christ, and I knew the Earth, Wind & Fire mission fit right into that spirit I received.

Larry Dunn explained to me the work of the early disciples in spreading Christianity and showed me how to speak in tongues. It was him and me in the room. Say what you want about Christianity, God, and Jesus Christ, but it is said that speaking in tongues is a manifestation of the Holy Spirit within you. When that happened to me, that was a moment. When you start, it just goes; only God hears your intent and can translate it.

Some things like miraculous healing are a God thing. The fact that I'm a cancer survivor is a God thing. In 2016, during the holiday season, I caught a cold, and my throat became hoarse. It never really went away. As I was having my regular lunch with my dear friend Richard Reiss, who was a fellow drummer in the Morningside High band and who is currently my chiropractor, he said, "You should check that out. I mean, anything after four days could be something more serious." I went to have my throat checked at the Osborne Head and Neck Institute at Cedars-Sinai, which my singer friend Howard Hewett recommended. Howard, who started as one of the lead singers in the group Shalamar and is now a solo artist, was very protective of managing his voice and urged me to go to his doctor, René Gupta, who saw me.

"There is something there," she told me, so we did a biopsy days later. Susie and I came back to her, and she confirmed, "I've got bad news. It's cancerous."

There was no sugarcoating. I was reminded of the bluntness that Maurice hit me with decades earlier, bringing my career to a screeching halt. We left stunned. The first call I made was to bandmates Verdine and Philip on a conference call.

They didn't hesitate in their reply. "Do what you gotta do. We got your back, Ralph. Whatever you need, we're here."

Susie and I were driving home thinking, *Where do we go from here? What do we do?* When the doctor tells you that you have the big C, you start thinking about all sorts of things. It's like your whole life flashes before you. How long do I have?

Dr. Gupta followed up with us, saying, "You know what, I've got a doctor back in Boston, Dr. Steven Zeitels. He's the best. I'm going to send your charts back to Boston and let him check them out. You'll have to fly to Boston." Susie and I flew to see Dr. Zeitels. He had pioneered this laser surgery where he scrapes cancer down to the core, and he had treated other A-list entertainers. He was very reassuring, "I got this."

I told him I had to do a tour in Europe with Lionel Richie. He reassuringly replied, "Go do your tour. When you get back, call me, and we will go to Mass General, and we'll knock this out."

While on tour, I shared my situation with Lionel, who assured me, too, that it would be okay. God had brought me the reassurance I needed that allowed me to focus on the tour. I really didn't worry about it.

When I returned from the tour, I had that surgery. After three weeks of vocal silence, I was good. I'm so grateful that I wasn't trying to come back from Stage 4 cancer. Mine was caught early, so it wasn't as bad as others have had to deal with. To this day, I thank God for Dr. Zeitels and his healing

Baby Ralph and his mom.
(J. Randolph Family Trust)

Ralph's dad.
(J. Randolph Family Trust)

The Classic Nine: Johnny Graham, Larry Dunn, Andrew Woolfolk, Al McKay, Maurice White, Philip Bailey, Verdine White, Fred White, and Ralph Johnson. (Getty)

Where it all started—Maverick's Flat. (Getty)

One of many group photos—this one from 1988 is during the *Touch The World* tour. *Pictured:* Verdine White, Sheldon Reynolds, Maurice White, Ralph Johnson, Philip Bailey, and Andrew Woolfolk. (Getty)

Displaying our well-rehearsed choreography, thank you to George Faison, our choreographer. Ralph Johnson with Larry Dunn, Maurice White, and Philip Bailey. (Getty)

An often-seen configuration of us—I would always be on Maurice's right! (Getty)

On tour in the Netherlands in the late ’70s. (Getty)

Ralph singing on tour with Earth, Wind & Fire and Chicago. (Getty)

Late '70s era. *Floor:* Fred White and Verdine White. *Middle:* Philip Bailey, Maurice White, and Ralph Johnson. *Top:* Al McKay, Larry Dunn, Johnny Graham, and Andrew Woolfolk. (Getty)

Maurice would often go into conductor mode and conduct the band. (Getty)

Dino and I doing what we do! (Getty)

Phil and me at Bonnaroo in 2015. (Getty)

On the video shoot for "Thinking of You" in 1987. (Getty)

Ralph and Maurice having a moment on stage. (Getty)

Backstage with Carlos Santana. (Getty)

Grammy Award–winning music producer Kizzo and Ralph on the HMMA Red Carpet. (Hollywood Music In Media Awards)

Verdine and Ralph hanging out with Clive Davis in NY. (Getty)

ASCAP Rhythm & Soul Awards in 2002. Ralph Johnson with Al McKay, Maurice White, Philip Bailey, and Verdine White. (Getty)

Induction ceremony at Guitar Center RockWalk in 2003. (Getty)

Philip, Ralph, and Verdine at the Grammys Red Carpet. (Getty)

Temecula Valley Music & Film Festival Music Lifetime Honorees in 2009. (Rhonda Bedikian)

Onstage in London in 2010. (Getty)

Keeping our fans engaged during the lockdown with DJ Cassidy as part of the virtual Parade Across America. (Getty)

At the Hollywood Bowl in 2025, Ralph performing "After the Love Has Gone" with Ray McKinley, David Whitworth, and Oshunde Bailey. (Getty)

Teaching is a passion! (Getty)

Kennedy Center Honorees in 2019. (Getty)

Ralph Johnson with his seven Grammys. (Rob Shanahan)

A special moment. (Mark-Anthony Johnson)

powers. When we were touring again later in 2019 and were in Boston, I visited Dr. Zeitels to thank him . . . again.

My New Year's resolution every year is quite simple—to be a better me and to be sensitive to the needs of others. I don't mind giving away money because my attitude about money is that there is always some more out there coming in. I don't have to pray on things like that because I know God is in control and taking care of me. God is my provider.

People tend to overemphasize the upside of celebrity entertainment life—the rich and famous lifestyle, the red carpets and awards shows, the financial benefits, houses, cars, cutting-edge fashion, never-ending relationship opportunities, the global travel, the access and exposure to seemingly the best of everything. After a half-century as a member of one of the most well-known, well-respected, and most commercially successful bands to take the stage, I still have something to relish: An Earth, Wind & Fire song is played somewhere in the world every ninety-eight seconds. I've had my share of success.

But reaping the material benefits of success is only part of the picture. My parents instilled in me as a child the lesson that to whom much is given, much is required. That has everything to do with sharing your success. Decades ago, I remember seeing the movie *Mahogany* with Billy Dee Williams and Diana Ross. Diana's character had become an overnight sensation, and her trappings of success so enthralled her that she set aside the relationship that had meant so much to her. Billy Dee, who was successful in his own right, reminded her in his dapper voice, "Success is nothing without having someone to share it with." I believe that. It's a strong point that should never be forgotten. The greatest joy is not in achieving success but in sharing it.

If Mom's house needed repairs, done. Floors needed carpeting, done. New appliances—oven, refrigerators, you name it, done.

I believe in giving and giving back and didn't want to keep my success to myself. I needed to see that others benefited.

But there were some challenges for me in trying to help others. There was some jealousy with my younger brother Fred. He was a musician with moderate talent and strongly felt I should have connected him to Earth, Wind & Fire. He had issues with my musical notoriety. I did my best to support him, buying equipment and instruments, but his jealousy did not subside. It may have been his plan to play with us, but that was not God's plan. Fred continued working at American Airlines, and his music career never took off like he imagined it might.

It wasn't always about buying friends and family material things; it wasn't always about giving money. Sometimes it was giving my time to be there and be a good listener.

Those close to me must share in my success. When I leave this earth, I don't want people to say, "Do you remember that guy in Earth, Wind & Fire who made all that money and played hit songs?" I want them to say, "Did you know Ralph Johnson? Because if you didn't know Ralph Johnson, you missed out on knowing a caring, sharing individual. His gift was felt in his spirit." You can't go through your life without knowing what's important. Maurice showed me this, balling up his fist and holding it out. "See that, Ralph, it's a closed fist. Nothing's getting out, and nothing's getting in. You gotta be open," he said as he opened his hand. "You gotta be a giver, and you gotta be a giver when you don't necessarily have it to give."

Now, that's the real deal there. Can I do that? Knowing that when I don't have it, but the other person needs it, I must give it up. I must be a giver. I subscribe to the mentality that one must give. I don't give because I am expecting something in return. I give because I know it's going to bless somebody. That's what is important to me. It's the law of reciprocation, the universal law. It will come back around. What you throw out there is what you're going to get. I'd rather give in love and grow in love.

We only have so much time on this earth to make a difference. In today's fast-paced world, it's easy to get caught up in the hustle and bustle of life and forget about people who matter most to us. But at the end of the day, it's not about how much money we have or how successful we are, but about our relationships with those around us. Taking time to be present with our loved ones, to listen to them, and to be there for them, is one of the greatest gifts we can give. It shows that we value and care about them; they are a priority in our lives. No amount of money or material possessions can replace the importance of a genuine human connection. I consciously prioritize the people I love and never let my success or busy schedule get in the way of those relationships.

Part Three

FIRE

Chapter 7

Business Is Business

Ralph has an incredible work ethic. He practices the drums daily and takes drum lessons. Yes, he still takes lessons even though he gives drum lessons to so many aspiring students and has written drum books. When he wants to know about something, he will study it, read about it, and practice until he masters it. That's how he got to where he is today . . . Ralph's relationship with the others [in EWF] is pretty laid-back . . . If he's needed on drums, he's there. As a percussionist, he's ready. When he's needed downstage as a vocalist, he's on point. He's there to support the entire group.

—Rhonda Bedikian, manager and publisher

Popularity ebbs and flows, but business is business. For all the attention I get as a celebrity member of Earth, Wind & Fire, I always remember that music is a business. It's how I earn my living. While some elements of the industry have changed with the advent of streaming and advanced technology delivery systems, artists still sign deals and are paid a percentage of the sales, whether from a major label or an independent one. For musicians, that royalty rate is important.

More artists coming up today understand the business of music better than most of us did back in the day. Being a successful artist requires a balance between creativity and business. Learning to be savvy about the business side of the industry shouldn't take away from an artist's creativity. Some artists think that a focus on commerce sullies their creations and thus have difficulty even thinking about getting involved in the business aspect of music. But these two aspects are inextricably bound. First, artists write songs because they're creative individuals, not just because they want to be in the business. The actual creation of a piece, the intellectual property, is the initial step of the process. Then, in order for an artist's lyrics and music to be widely heard, the record label must market and distribute the song. How that piece is distributed or marketed is the business side of the process, which involves turning a song into a stream of revenue for the label.

I now tell aspiring musicians that if they are going to be a part of a group, they need to be a writer so they can still make money long after the touring stops, but when people continue to buy and listen to their records. When I realized that writing and publishing were central to success in the music business, I knew I needed to start writing songs myself or co-writing with others.

In 1990, I finally started engaging with Maurice on the writing end. There was this loose process of getting your song on an EWF album. Ultimately, Maurice decided whether or not a song would make the record, so every song idea was given to, or shared with, Maurice for him to consider. When we submitted a song to Reece, it wasn't necessarily complete. We didn't always come to him with a polished arrangement or a fully written set of lyrics or score. It might just be a track he was in love with. I remember Al McKay would often be at sound check and would play a groove, and Maurice would say, "What's that?" The next thing I knew, they had developed that groove into a song. You could submit a song idea, and Maurice would vibe on it for a while and say, "Let's do something with that."

The first song I wrote with Maurice was entitled "Welcome," which was on our final album on Columbia/CBS, *Heritage*. I went to Maurice and said, "Let's get together and do some writing." He showed me the tune for "Welcome," but he needed some lyrics, so I said, "Let me help you write some lyrics." We started working on those together. For me, it was a creative motivation and a financial motivation. I had kids, and I was always thinking of ways to create another revenue stream or at least broaden it. I continued to write interludes. Maurice was into interludes. If I came up with the right musical idea, I knew he'd go for it. That was my way into working with Maurice as a writer.

My writing partner, Marcel East, the younger brother of world-class bassist Nathan East, and I penned multiple tunes together. My favorite interlude was called "Avatar." Maurice liked that title so much, he named the album *Avatar*, which was released in Japan in 1996 and then reissued internationally in 2006 as *In the Name of Love*. "Avatar" was one of my favorites because it's not in the regular time signature. It's written in 11/8. I wanted to do it differently because one of my favorite jazz tunes, "Follow Your Heart" by John McLaughlin, is written in 11/8. John's always breaking boundaries and barriers by doing things in a way that takes you to a different place, and he asks you to come along with him while he's doing that. He's an inspiration for me and someone I listen to, and he, with others like Thom Bell, who wrote all those Delfonics hits, helped shape my writing. Thom was an incredible arranger, and he helped get me started on the writing side. As much as I love jazz, I am influenced by R&B music because it's easier for me to get to lyrically. When you think about jazz, you're thinking basically instrumental pieces, but lyrically, R&B is it. But I love them both.

I waited fifteen albums before I contributed my songs to an EWF album. That's the one professional regret I have. I should have started writing for EWF sooner. It seems crazy now when I think that I lost valuable time and revenue because I didn't focus on the business side early. I did consistently contribute songs to future albums, including two songs—an interlude, "Belo Horizonte," and a full song, "Got to Be Love"—to our twentieth album, *Now, Then & Forever,* which peaked at No. 6 on the Top R&B/Hip-Hop Albums. We were trying to maintain that EWF sound we had all along on this album. When I submitted "Got to Be Love," our keyboardist Myron McKinley was listening to it, and he took part of what I submitted and created another song around it. Sometimes, with a song, you might not like the A section, but you love the B section, so you write around that and create a whole new song.

I was happy because my creativity led to another revenue stream as a writer. I now make money as a writer, own my publishing, and have the copyright to my songs. Sometimes, a song you write never gets sampled. But you keep writing, you keep sharing what's in your heart, what's on your mind. That's what I did in those eight years between *The Promise* album in 2005 and *Now, Then & Forever* in 2013.

While I had been writing regularly even before I joined Earth, Wind & Fire, I had not been attentive to the business of music. I was content with the money I was making just touring and playing live, but I noticed Maurice, Phil, Al, and Verdine were also making publishing money for songs they wrote. I was writing songs, just not for EWF albums. Just like a visual artist sketches every day, writers must write. I wrote songs for the album *Bobby Glenn: Shout It Out* (1976), with Douglas Gibbs, who recently passed away. Irv Kessler, who was producing then, asked us to do an album for Bobby Glenn and his brother, Gary Glenn. Even though I had just joined Earth, Wind & Fire, I finished this album that I had already started in 1972. It included the song "Sounds Like a Love Song," which went on to become my biggest piece of passive income that was not related to EWF.

I was enjoying the EWF life, so I didn't give that album or song much thought. Then, in the summer of 2001, I got a very unexpected phone call from this attorney in New York who said to me, "Ralph Johnson, you have been sampled."

I replied, "Okay, who sampled me?"

The attorney says, "Jay-Z."

I exclaimed, "Whaat!"

I couldn't believe it! Jay-Z's attorney had just called and shared that the song I wrote and had appeared earlier on an obscure album some thirty years ago was being sampled. I always wondered if my music would get sampled one day, and then it happened. That song, "Song Cry," is on Jay-Z's sixth album, *The Blueprint*, which debuted at No. 1 and is two-times multiplatinum.

There was no sampling when I wrote "Sounds Like a Love Song" in 1972. Jay-Z, Drake, Keisha Cole, and Queen Naija have now sampled it, and it won the 2023 ASCAP Rhythm & Soul Music Award on Queen Naija's album *Hate Our Love*. That one song continues to be sampled and generates significant personal revenue because I am always included in the "splits," the determination of who receives what percentage of royalties for a song. Ron Isley and Swizz Beatz sampled "Sounds Like a Love Song" for the TV show *The Godfather of Harlem*, starring Forest Whitaker.

I will never sell my catalog of music for the very reason that I don't know how it might be received or used in the future. Big artists sell their catalogs for different reasons. You don't know what's going on in their minds. Some likely do need the money. But some say, "Look, they are offering me so much money." Even when some do sell their catalog, if a deal is done right, they are still going to get a percentage of what's coming in. Not a large percentage, but if it's a large active catalog, they will still get a percentage of what's going on. On the publishing side, if what's called a royalty override deal is made, no matter what the terms are, writers still get their cut as the creator.

Those are some of the reasons why someone would sell their catalog. For example, the ATV Music Publishing catalog containing only Lennon–McCartney compositions was sold to Michael Jackson in 1985 for $47.5 million. I don't know all the inner workings of that deal, though I do know that it was Paul McCartney who told Michael about the auction of the Beatles' catalog. Of course, he was never expecting that Michael would be the one to purchase it, that he had that much money in hand. Paul felt betrayed, but it was a hell of a deal for Michael.

Sony and CBS oversee Michael Jackson's music catalog, and they watch over the Earth, Wind & Fire catalog, too, which Maurice's estate controls. Maurice's son Kahbran runs the EWF brand now. To this day, my writing partner Douglas Gibbs's royalty portion goes to his estate, where his sister is in charge. I have so much appreciation, respect, and love for Rhonda Bedikian, my manager and publishing administrator, who, I like to say, knows where all the bodies are buried. She helped Douglas Gibbs and me negotiate our "Sounds Like a Love Song" sample. She also helped Doug's sister, Sandra Gibbs, together with an attorney, get all that she deserved. Doug was part of Billy Preston's group and sang background, but I met Doug at Maverick's Flat when I was a part of The Master's Children. We took an interest in writing and just wrote and wrote songs. How could we know back then that something we wrote in the 1970s would still be relevant in the next century? That's why it's important to get involved in the creative process because artists never know if something they have created, this intellectual property—a song, a movie script, a book, an idea for a TV show—will result in huge benefits.

Life in the music business can be fast-paced, yet routine. Compose songs. Go to the studio. Produce the album. Do the promo. Go on tour. Rinse and repeat. To maintain creativity and energy, musicians engage in other activities related to the music business. During our EWF hiatus, for example, Al McKay and I produced The Temptations in 1983. Maurice took producing to another level. He had a production deal with CBS and his own label to produce other artists. Did he ever! He produced Deniece Williams's album *This Is Niecy*, which rose to No. 3 on the US Billboard Top Soul Albums on the strength of the single "Free," and he went on to produce her next three well-received albums, including a duet album featuring Johnny Mathis and Deniece.

Soon, the Emotions signed under his label, and Reece produced their gold album *Flowers*, which rose to No. 5 on the Top 100 Soul Albums with the dance track "I Don't Want to Lose Your Love." The Emotions' next album, *Rejoice*, peaked at No. 1 on the US *Billboard* R&B chart and No. 7 on the US *Billboard* Top 20 chart; the album is certified as platinum. *Rejoice* featured the singles "The Best of My Love" and "Don't Ask My Neighbors." Maurice continued producing the Emotions albums and eventually connected the Emotions with Earth, Wind & Fire in the massive gold single hit "Boogie

Wonderland," which rose to No. 2 on the US Hot Soul singles chart, No. 6 on the US *Billboard* Hot 100, and No. 14 on the UK Singles Chart.

Maurice's producer skills continued to grant him more notoriety and great success. He produced his former bandmate and the jazz great Ramsey Lewis multiple times, including his No. 1 *Sun Goddess* album, whose single was also featured on our *Gratitude* album. The song "Can't Hide Love," on that same album, was such an impactful song that we remade it with Lucky Daye in 2021 as "You Want My Love."

* * *

In 2021, we had the honor of collaborating with the exceedingly talented Kenny "Babyface" Edmonds, along with the vocal stylings of Lucky Daye.

The song? "Can't Hide Love" reimagined! Soon to become "You Want My Love" by Earth, Wind & Fire with a Babyface production? Loved it!

The video was a club setting. Phil, Verdine, and I were the house band, and we invited Lucky up to a number. At the end of the video, it went to live sound, and everyone was singing the vamp to "Can't Hide Love." You know the one. Lucky Daye laid it out, end of story.

* * *

"Can't Hide Love" from the *Gratitude* album was a hit among many, but Maurice was in a producing zone. He scored big in producing the platinum Barbara Streisand album *Emotion* and Jennifer Holiday's Grammy-nominated album that featured the single "I Am Love," and he also produced the gospel great Walter Hawkins, Neil Diamond, and Pieces of a Dream, among so many others.

During Maurice's producer run, no EWF members were included on his production team. I had a tune on Philip's *Chinese Wall* album and played on the Larry Dunn Orchestra album, but none of Reece's. I did not dwell on working with Maurice during this time. He was doing his thing, and I was proud of his success.

I started my own production company, V12 Productions, in 2000, when I went to Copenhagen, Denmark, to embark on a new jazz conceptual project. Morris Pleasure, Steen Kyed, and I put together a group we called Audio Caviar. We started recording in Denmark and then brought the album back to the States, where production continued with my other writing partner Marcel East, with whom I had co-written the song "Go" that was on Philip's *Chinese Wall* album. Our recording process worked this way: We'd write the song. I'd be on drums, and Mo would be on bass, and we would record that. Then Mo would come back and lay on the piano. We released the album called *Transoceanic* (2000), which featured guest artists including my friend Howard Hewett, Jonathan Butler, George Duke, and Philip Bailey, my EWF bandmate.

Its positive reception encouraged me to move further into the jazz space. I was still with Earth, Wind & Fire, which was highly successful as Maurice's program, but I was now excited about what I could create. What else did I have to say musically? I was working with my longtime friend, writer Raymond Crossley, who could move me more into a smooth jazz direction. I had my promo people—Ted Joseph, Cliff and Jason Goroff—who could aid in helping make that transition. It was just a matter of coming up with the right song and putting it out there. In 2019, I released "Co-Swagit (Everything's Cool)." Then, in March 2020, right when the pandemic started, I recorded "Smooth and You," the tune I put out with Gerald Clayton that Crossley and I produced. Both efforts were well received by the jazz community, charting in the Jazz Top 30.

I was then working with EWF on our Christmas album and didn't feel deeply involved. Raymond brought in this track that I liked, and I created the hook "Have a Very Merry Christmas" on it. We had worked with Siedah Garrett, who wrote Michael Jackson's "Man in the Mirror." I wondered if Siedah would work with me in writing this Christmas song. I was a little intimidated because she was such a great songwriter, but without hesitation, she said, "Yes," and she wrote the lyrics to our music entitled "Have a Very Merry Christmas," which was featured in the 2019 film *Holiday Rush*. I later added horns by John Clayton, my youngest son's father-in-law, which is the version you hear today.

I have always tried to keep my music current over the years. It's easy to become stagnant when you are always playing power playlists with a group like Earth, Wind & Fire, so stretching yourself now and then with other music is good. Even during our EWF peak, I guest appeared on Blue Magic's *Message from the Magic* album in 1979. Skip Scarborough called and asked me to play drums on the tracks. It was a lot of fun. Then, I was able to jump into some jazz with Stanley Turrentine on his 1981 *Tender Togetherness*, where I did some percussion work. I had the chance to play some jazz, my first love, with Turrentine, one of my favorite sax players.

I produced Howard Hewett's 2008 Christmas album with Monty Seward and Howard, who had not done a Christmas album at that date. I played drums on the tracks I produced and called on fellow musicians Myron McKinley, Greg "G-Mo" Moore, and my EWF brother, Verdine White. We just had a wonderful time groovin' together. The Christmas chemistry happened again in 2019 when EWF performed on Meghan Trainor's Christmas album video.

In some ways, doing these additional guest artist gigs are all in a day's work, but when I'm on the production side, I'm learning more because every producer has his tricks of the trade you can learn from. I enjoy the creative process, period. It's one thing to sit down at a piano and create a song, but it's another thing to go into the studio and make it come to life. I enjoy the production. That's why I enjoyed working with Al McKay when we worked with the Temptations.

In 2020, Jon Batiste, who was the musical director on *The Late Show with Stephen Colbert,* and his producer Kizzo, asked me to play percussion for one of his tracks. It was Verdine on the bass and me. Then, he asked me to do vocals, and

I said, "Yeah, sure," since I don't get asked for my vocals very often. Always jump on opportunities to strengthen yourself as a musician.

You never know what will happen when you try something different. It was 2011 when the CEO/Head of School Rory Pullens of the Duke Ellington School of the Arts in Washington, DC, asked Earth, Wind & Fire to be a part of their Legends Series of Performances held at the John F. Kennedy Center to help raise resources for the next generation of Black artists.

I'm thinking, "This is a high school. Really?"

Their Legend series had already featured comedian and alum of the school, Dave Chappelle; the opera star and alum of the school, Denyce Graves; Stevie Wonder; Patti LaBelle; and Smokey Robinson, and would go on to host legends Sting and Paul Simon. EWF was celebrating our fortieth anniversary at the time, and the Duke Ellington School was celebrating its fortieth. It turned out to be a perfect fit. We performed to a sold-out audience, generated $750,000 for the students, and something happened I never expected: a side door opened for me to further develop my passion, arts education. Pullens asked if we would stop by the school the next day and give a master class for the students—Phil on vocal music, Verdine on guitar, and me on drums. Interestingly enough, I had just written a drum book for drum students, though I had never really promoted it. I thought it would be cool to come back and continue working with the drummers/percussionists at Duke Ellington. Every time I was in DC, I stopped by the school and did just that. The drum instructor started using my book as a reference for students. After a while, I was simply Uncle Ralph. Not the celebrity, not the EWF star, just a drumming mentor and teacher. I was able to impact young artists' lives. I cannot overstate why the educational side of the arts is so important.

I recently went back to my old high school, Morningside High in Inglewood, with my longtime friend, Richard Reiss, who tells it best. "There were no instruments, no music, and we went to a room where there should have been instruments, but instead, it was a pile of rubble. The next week Ralph shows up and brings in drumstick sets, music books, music stands, and drum pads for the entire class. Then, he said he would teach the percussion class. Watching him teach, he not only has a passion for teaching, but is one of the greatest teachers I've ever seen."

One door opens another. Back in 2014, EWF was on tour in Europe, and I mentioned to Nick Stewart, the person who handled us in the London area, that I had always wanted to be a broadcaster on the air and wanted to do a jazz show because growing up as a kid in LA, we had the first 24-hour jazz station on KBCA 105.1 FM.

Nick said, "Sure," and called a friend to arrange that at BBC Radio. I did four hours of programming twice at NPR Studios in Los Angeles on Jefferson Boulevard. I brought in my playlist, the producer and I sat together, and we just started playing jazz. It was so successful that it started my broadcasting career. I was just emulating the cool music from my childhood and did what those deejays did. Then, after starting our residency at the Venetian in Vegas, I was asked to do an interview at KUNV 91.5 on the campus of UNLV. The operations manager, Jason Beaty, loved the way I sounded and offered me a slot at the station. I am now going on four years, and I love it.

I'm in my fourth year at KUNV 91.5 and thoroughly enjoy it. My show—*The Jazz Epicenter*, the finest in jazz from the '60s and '70s—airs 8 to 10 P.M. Pacific time every Saturday night. I've done well over 120 shows now. Listeners dig my playlist and have occasionally commented on the overall vibe of the show. It's a great musical look back to FM jazz radio in the '60s and '70s. Listeners talk about the show's creativity, but the programming's everything I heard while growing up in LA listening to KBCA 105.1. I usually record the show in my home studio in Los Angeles, but because I'm on the road quite a bit still, I travel with my recording equipment and do it in hotel rooms across the nation. It's quite compact—my MacBook, my interface, my mics. It's gratifying to do the business I do because I love it.

Celebrity is often a double-edged sword. When you are a celebrity, people often think that you should say yes to everything you're asked to do and that you always have the time and should be there for them how they want you to be. That's just not true. I must pick and choose the projects I want to get involved in. That is an advantage of being a celebrity. My reputation precedes me with a group that has been on top for fifty years. I don't think about it much, but every now and then, I will play the Earth, Wind & Fire card to, if you will, expedite things.

Life is too short to be restricted, to stay in our comfort zones. I'm ready to try some new areas and new things. My new frontier is television and film production. I'd like to produce some of the projects I have been involved in developing: *Uncle Ralph's House*, *F Street Kidz*, *Christmas Reunion*, and some new ideas I have. Just like there's some unreleased Earth, Wind & Fire music sitting in the vaults that you may one day hear or never hear, there is content that I have started working on and would like to get out there eventually.

My participation in Earth, Wind & Fire and its spin-off opportunities consumed my life, as it did my bandmates'. It's what I did. It's what we all did; it's what we all had and looked forward to. It didn't matter how big or how small. The joy was being in the music, growing as a creator, and being creative.

Whether it is me being featured or the group being the center of our fans' attention, our music from the early 1970s plays just as well today as it did then. Our phone is still ringing. Our music is still uplifting. It appeals to the human spirit to make it better. I will always cherish the Earth, Wind & Fire memories and my bandmates, but all my non-EWF professional friendships are equally valued, and there are many friendships and relationships that still exist today.

The music industry can be unpredictable, and success in the industry only sometimes guarantees financial stability. However, individuals can do a few things to increase their chances of making a living as a musician: (1) Diversify income streams:

Don't rely solely on music sales or streaming revenue. Explore other sources of income, such as merchandise sales, sync licensing, and live performances; (2) Network and collaborate: Build relationships with other musicians and industry professionals. Collaborate with other artists, attend industry events, and use social media to connect; (3) Keep current on industry trends and changes. Learn about different revenue streams and explore new ways to monetize music. The music industry is constantly evolving, so be willing to adapt to changes and explore new opportunities as they arise.

Looking back, one of the things we never really dug into as a band—not the way we should have—was money. Not just getting it . . . but *keeping it.* And more importantly, *growing it.* We never sat around and talked about investing or long-term financial strategy. Sure, I remember Maurice—always a sharp, forward-thinking brother—saying a few things early on about T-bills, Treasury bills. He had a sense that putting money somewhere safe was the right thing to do, and I appreciated him pulling me aside to share that. But outside of that moment? Nothing too in-depth.

There weren't many detailed discussions about stock portfolios, mutual funds, or even real estate. No real talk about precious metals or compound interest or building generational wealth. Not because we weren't smart. We were. But we were so caught up in *the music,* in the moment, in keeping up with the whirlwind of touring, recording, and building the brand, that we never slowed down to ask: "What are we doing with all this money?" But making money isn't the same as knowing what to do with it.

You see it over and over again in the entertainment world—in sports, in music, in film. Talented individuals, at the top of their game, signing massive contracts and bringing in revenue most people only dream about . . . only to wake up one day and it's *gone*. They're struggling to pay taxes on homes they no longer own.

Why? Because no one taught them how to manage wealth. No one pulled us aside and said, "This is how you make your money work for you."

"This is how you build income that doesn't rely on you showing up."

I wish we'd had those conversations. Not just among the band, but around us—managers, lawyers, accountants, people who could've said, "Hey, you should own a piece of this publishing." Or "Let's diversify that tour money before it dries up."

But here's what I've come to understand, and what I try to share with the next generation of musicians: Active income is temporary. Passive income is forever.

Some artists are shocked when I tell them: It's better to own 10 percent of a hit you wrote than to get paid 100 percent to perform someone else's music. One brings applause. The other brings royalties. You want to be on the writing side, on the publishing side. That's where the music industry hides the long-term value.

The music industry brings in billions every year. Every platform—Spotify, Apple Music, TikTok, TV shows, commercials—all of it is built on licensed music. And that licensing goes back to whoever holds the publishing. *That's* who gets paid—every time the music is played, streamed, or synced.

So yes, I've had the blessing of being part of one of the greatest musical legacies in modern history. But if I could go back and tell my younger self something? It wouldn't just be, "Keep playing hard." It would be, "Own your work. Understand your rights. Ask questions. Think long-term. And never assume the money will last forever."

And for the artists reading this—the aspiring musicians, the garage band dreamers, the producers making beats in their bedrooms, know this: Don't just chase a deal. Chase ownership. Don't just play the gig. Learn the business. Don't just hope you'll make money. Make sure you know how to grow it.

Because at the end of the day, the spotlight dims. The stage lights fade. And if you're lucky, you'll still have something left to show for all the years you gave to your craft.

I'm still learning. Still exploring. Still expanding. And while I'm grateful for the life I've lived and the career I've had, I know now: Success isn't just about how high you fly.

It's about where you land—and whether you built something that lasts.

In my early years, I'd say, "I'm going on tour now, so I guess I'll make some money." Yeah, but what about when I came off the road? Was there a check coming in from ASCAP or BMI waiting for me because I wrote something?

I'm fortunate, I do live a good life. Not a super extravagant one, but I am more than comfortable. If there is something I want, I can go get it. Sure, I can buy super elaborate material things that would make people say "Wow," but I have seen too many examples of people who have gone before me in this business making the wrong decisions, and I didn't want to be one of them. It's that simple. I know a famous musician who had a group, conquered Woodstock, and ended up selling all his publishing rights because he had a serious substance abuse problem. He just gave away all his wealth.

I am fortunate to have music as my business. My wealth, however, goes far beyond my accomplishments in music. Every person needs to consider their economic status in larger terms, not just their job, but in investments.

I think it's important to come up with a plan. I am very fortunate and blessed because I write songs that create revenue, and once that song is out there and selling, that is passive income. But at the same time, I go on tour with Earth, Wind & Fire, and that's active income. I am fortunate to have the best of both worlds. It's beneficial to create both. We can't just live on the consumer side of economics where we long to buy this, we live to buy that. We are destined to fail if we don't snap out of that mentality. There's a saying, "If you fail to plan, then you plan to fail." We all must have a plan.

I was told, "Once you get off the main road and make a left turn, getting back to the main road can be tough." How many superstar artists didn't have a lot when they passed away? So many are overly extravagant at the peak of their commercial success, choosing to live the opulent life, but what financial legacy do they leave their families? There are so many examples of those who didn't figure it out. They had no guidance, didn't choose to listen, or thought they had more time. They did it their own way and lost. I'm not going to be one of those. I'm going to enjoy my life and the fruits of my labor, but I'm also going to figure some stuff out and make some sound decisions about how I want to invest to ensure the financial legacy of my family.

Chapter 8

To Boldly Do What I've Never Done Before

He has not only a passion for teaching but is one of the greatest teachers I've ever seen . . . He has a gift, an incredible teacher, a professor with incredible charisma . . . Ralph touches people's lives in ways he does not know.

—Richard Reiss, high school friend,
chiropractor, musician

Being in Earth, Wind & Fire has taken me around the world, and while I continue to write songs and perform to enthusiastic fans in sold-out arenas around the world, I have always tried to grow beyond my music and pursue other interests that would expand my cultural knowledge and challenge me physically and spiritually. Over the past fifty years, I have developed a love of art and acquired a large collection that reflects my taste and artistic passions. In addition, I have dived the depths of the oceans as a scuba diver, soared through air as a pilot, and worked out my mental and physical stress through karate.

The Art Collection

Those who have visited my home in Southern California's Woodland Hills community, just outside of Los Angeles, often say it's more like a museum. I'd say it's more like an art gallery than just a humble abode showcasing furniture and plants. I wouldn't have it any other way.

Most are immediately drawn to my Earth, Wind & Fire collection of pictures and artifacts scattered about from room to room. My six Grammy Awards and a Grammy Lifetime Achievement Award sit on the fireplace mantel in the comfortable den while the living room showcases my Kennedy Center Honors medallion with plaques and pictures of Philip, Verdine, and me on that memorable occasion. A cabinet of Earth, Wind & Fire vinyl records from over the past fifty years is stacked neatly to be played on the ample stereo system, just waiting to be cranked up. Lining the stairwell walls is an impressive and stunning sampling of gold and platinum records from our various hits, framed posters of key concerts and performances, and pictures with various industry people important to me. Nestled downstairs is my recording studio where I tape my weekly radio show and other musical endeavors, along with two drum sets I use for practice and teaching lessons to those in the community. It's clear that my home is a mini-museum showcasing my career, but yet, it is almost overshadowed by my art collection, which has also been nearly fifty years in the making.

While I can't give you the exact number, my collection includes hundreds of eclectic pieces. I have yet to catalog some of it, and a new appraisal will increase its collective value. My collection comes from different places all around the world and represents multiple styles. Certain things will speak to my spirit when I am out in galleries or private shows, and that's what I will get. Art has a powerful emotional impact on my soul and evokes various feelings and thoughts. This awareness is what guides me when selecting artwork to acquire. Building a collection of pieces that are meaningful to me and reflect my personal taste and style is what it's all about. Ultimately when I bring art home, I must live with it. There are no boundaries, zones, or genres of what I'm looking for. It just must be something I love. Like in music, I'm looking to be moved. Whether it's Victor Vasarely and his optical art look or the self-taught Black artist based in Atlanta, Frank Morrison, whose works are steeped in family and community values, my collection will continue to grow.

In 1976 I thought it would be interesting to get into limited-edition graphics, so I started looking around and buying magazines that had to do with art. There was a gallery on Ventura Boulevard called Art Dimensions near my house in Sherman Oaks. On a recommendation from a friend, I purchased pieces by Victor Vasarely, the Hungarian-French artist who is considered "The Father of the Optical Art Movement." I love that visual art style using optical illusions, giving the impression of movement, flashing and vibrating patterns, and hidden images. The colorful chess set prominently featured in my living room is Vasarely, as you can tell by its optical illusion graphic design.

I went full in on Vasarely's pieces and started buying his and other major artwork both locally and internationally in 1977, 1978, and 1979. I was especially fond of the Shiseido Gallery in Tokyo, Japan. And then my art dealer in DC, Meech Lareuse, helped me purchase Chagall lithograph books, which I'm constantly in pursuit of.

My growing collection extends to other artists including the LA area artist Neal Doty from Glendale, whose drawing, painting, etching, and printmaking show influences of Picasso's cubism period to the works of Matisse and Dali. Over the years, I have continued to educate myself by studying the artists and their works. My art collection now includes African sculpture and pottery pieces from the Rookwood art pottery company that started in the late 1800s in Cincinnati, Ohio.

My Earth, Wind & Fire bandmates are certainly aware of my passion for my art collection, but they did not share in it, except maybe Verdine, who got into the art collection world when we were in Tokyo, and I took him to the Shiseido Gallery. He was surprised by the depth of conversation I was having about the art and was blown away by it. Verdine now has quite a collection of his own.

Art collecting will always be important to me because everyone needs something outside of furniture and plants to enhance the home environment. I may be a musical artist, but my love for the arts goes far beyond that.

Into the Ocean Depths

When I was a child, I became enamored with scuba diving by watching Lloyd Bridges on television in his weekly show, *Sea Hunt*. I was fascinated by it, and even back then I thought I would one day explore the ocean's depths.

It was 1976, and I lived alone in my Sherman Oaks home. I woke up one morning and said, "You know what? I'm gonna check out a scuba diving course." Just like that. I did the same thing with martial arts not long after.

The shop was called Scuba Duba Dive. I walked in, told them what I wanted, and they said, "Yes, we can do that. We can make you into a scuba diver." My instructor's name was Steve Maderas, and he was excellent as I completed the beginning course in four weeks to receive my beginner's certification. Steve challenged me, "If you do three more weeks, you can get the Advanced Open Water Certification." Without hesitation, I accepted the challenge. I now have an NAUI (National Association of Underwater Instructors) Advanced Open Water Certification. I'm also nitrox certified, the special gas we breathe that allows a diver longer bottom times because of a lesser nitrogen concentration and more oxygen in the mix.

I still go diving whenever I have time. The last time I was out was in January 2023 in Cozumel, Mexico, and it was the greatest vacation of my life. It was 80 degrees in the crystal-clear water. It doesn't get much better than that. I've been to Honolulu, Hawaii, and Hanauma Bay, off the island of Oahu.

A great spot is Roatan, about forty miles off the coast of Honduras, and I've been to one of the revered spots in Cozumel, Mexico.

In Cozumel, my typical dive day goes like this: I get up in the morning and have a little breakfast. The dive operation was right there next to my hotel, and all I had to do was walk out the back of my room fifty feet to it. I get my gear on the boat. They had three or four different boats going out to different locations. We were all diving off Palancar Reef, which runs for miles and miles with different coral formations. We got on the boat for what would be a two-tank dive. We made our first dive early in the morning in the 80-degree water. I was on a wreck dive. Others would be on a drop-off where the reef just plunges three hundred feet down, and you just kind of cruise down. During my wreck dive, I saw an old boat that was just sitting down there. I circled it, snapping pictures with my underwater camera. Most of these dives are drift dives because the current just takes you along, so you don't do a lot of kicking. When my air level reached a certain point, I started making my way to the surface, stopping at fifteen feet for three minutes. Sometimes things don't work as scheduled, so there are hand signs you can flash if you have low air pressure in your tank or are out of air.

On the dive, I see sharks, turtles, and sea eels. Sharks are not trying to get me, the opposite of what most people think from watching movies like *Jaws*. There are beautiful sting rays. They can be dangerous if you step on them. They will pop you and get your attention. The corals are beautiful, and I see all the sea life. It's so relaxing to get away from all the hustle and bustle and be alone underwater with the sound of my bubbles in this underwater landscape. Diving is great as it lowers my blood pressure in this serene settling. Diving is one of the coolest things I ever learned how to do.

Flight Time

I have always wanted to be a pilot. As a child I was inspired by the TV show *Sky King*. The show's star was the actor Kirby Grant, who played a pilot who flew a twin-engine Cessna. Another show that kept me interested in flying as a child was *12 O'Clock High*. I was attracted to anything that had to do with airplanes. Even today, I love military aircraft and the history around them. The aircraft that turned World War II around for the United States was the P-51. The updated P-51 is the plane the Red Tails, the Tuskegee Airmen, flew. Our military leaders didn't think Black airmen could fly. We proved them wrong. We were so good at flying the P-51s that the white bomber pilots would request the Tuskegee Airmen to accompany them. The Tuskegee Airmen never lost a battle, never fled a fight. Other airmen would turn around and get out of the way, but not the Red Tails. That's why they are remembered so honorably in history. They are another reason I wanted to fly.

As serious as flying is—and don't get me wrong, it *is* serious—I've managed to have my share of fun in the air. I even told one particularly hilarious (and very true) story at Maurice's memorial service, and judging by the stunned looks on my bandmates' faces that day, they had *definitely* never heard this one before.

You see, what none of them knew—not Philip, not Verdine, *not even Maurice*—was that I once flew a plane with the entire Earth, Wind & Fire band on board. Yep. Every last one of them, fast asleep, cruising thousands of feet above the ground, completely unaware that their drummer had taken the wheel—or the yoke, in this case.

We were somewhere over the clouds, flying to our next show, when Duke Morton—our regular captain and the guy who'd been giving me flying lessons—leaned out from the cockpit, gave me a look, and signaled with that classic "come on up" nod. Duke always had a cool confidence about him, like he'd just stepped out of a jazz club, and he used to joke, "If you can do those wild drum rotations on stage, you can fly a plane. It's all rhythm and coordination, baby."

I always sat close to the front of the plane—usually next to Maurice—partly because I liked being near the action, and partly because I always thought, if something ever goes wrong, at least I'm in jumping distance of the cockpit. Thankfully, this time there was no emergency. Just Duke, grinning and giving me a once-in-a-lifetime chance.

Now, this wasn't some rinky-dink plane. This was a big, British-made, four-engine turboprop called a Viscount. A real beast. Up until that point, I'd only flown smaller planes—little single-engine birds like the Piper Warrior. Light, maneuverable, like the sports cars of the sky. But this Viscount? This thing was a flying tour bus. Heavy, loud, majestic. It took a minute to get used to the feel of it—the sluggish response of the controls, the deep hum of all that power pushing through the sky.

There was no autopilot. Duke wanted me to *feel* the plane.

So, there I was, gripping the controls, cruising at altitude, and for a moment, it hit me: I was literally flying Earth, Wind & Fire. My hands were on the yoke, the weight of the band—musically and physically—was in my hands, and everyone, including Maurice, was knocked out cold in their seats. Not a soul stirred.

The absurdity of it made me want to laugh right there in the cockpit, but I was too busy keeping us steady. The thrill? Oh, man. It wasn't just adrenaline—it was a kind of quiet euphoria, like being in perfect sync with something much bigger than yourself. I'd experienced a lot of highs onstage, but that night, in that cockpit, I found a new kind of high. Quite literally.

Nobody knew. Not for years.

I held on to that secret until Maurice's memorial service. I shared the story from the stage, and I watched the guys' eyes grow wide—some with disbelief, others with dawning horror, like they were just realizing they'd once unknowingly been passengers on *my* maiden flight in a turboprop. And when I told them everyone had been asleep, including Maurice, who snored through the whole thing right next to me . . . Well, let's just say the room cracked up—and maybe clenched up—all at once.

That flight opened up something new in me. It broadened my horizons, both metaphorically and literally. I still haven't finished all the steps to get my pilot's license, but I plan to. One day soon, I'll be certified to fly solo.

And who knows—maybe I'll be the one flying Earth, Wind & Fire to our next gig. Though something tells me *that* might be the one flight where nobody dares fall asleep.

Hittin' Back with Martial Arts

It was 1976. Karate was something I also wanted to do from watching all those Bruce Lee movies. Who didn't watch the karate master Bruce Lee kick butt back in the day? His movie *Enter the Dragon* inspired legions of youth to jump into the martial arts craze. My mind jolted back to the times I was bullied in elementary school and how I wished I had real skills to fight back then, Bruce Lee style.

While my Earth, Wind & Fire bandmates did not participate in this hobby with me, I must admit the first time I heard about Kung Fu San Soo was from Al McKay, our guitarist, who started taking lessons but never took them all the way through. However, I couldn't start something and not finish, so I had to see it to the end and became a black belt. I started to study the fascinating style of Kung Fu San Soo in 1998. I just kept at it and am now a third-degree black belt in it, and a first-degree black belt in Tang Soo Do.

My Kung Fu San Soo instructor is Master Paul Borisoff and, additionally, my karate instructors were Mark Zacharatos and Ron Pohnel. To this day, I credit Mark and Ron for turning me into a fighter. I'm a black belt in two styles—Kung

Fu San Soo and Tang Soo Do. April 7, 1984, is etched in my mind as it was the day I became a black belt. I never felt so much pressure as when I had to take that test. Preparation started six months in advance—forms, fighting, one steps, board breaking, the whole arsenal of skills. I used to go out to tournaments and fight. There were always some tournaments going on. I learned the art quickly and did well as a fighter.

Going to a tournament and fighting on the weekends would be nothing for me. Weekend after weekend, fight after fight, I was determined to succeed. The most memorable was winning that first trophy. The place didn't matter. I had this mentality when I was tournament fighting that once I knew I had placed—it didn't matter first, second, or third—I didn't care. I knew I had won a trophy, so I'd just back off. I wasn't trying to destroy people then. I just wanted to polish my skills as a fighter.

Martial arts gave me confidence and self-awareness. It triggered commitment and self-discipline. These four qualities are a must to be successful. Today, I'm very confident. When I auditioned for EWF, I was confident. Just like with martial arts, I said, "Let's go!" Don't be afraid to step out and try something new. I carry myself a certain way with my head up, shoulders back, and looking straight ahead. I won't tolerate any bullying or intimidation. At the end of the night, when I take my final bow on "September," I do my San Soo salute as a nod to martial artists everywhere. My bow is different, I know, but there's always a smile on my face when I do it.

I've always leaned toward structure. Toward the kind of discipline that isn't rigid but *anchored*. Calm in chaos. That's how I was trained—not just in the dojo, but in life. That's how I approach everything—music, relationships, the stage, the studio, the world.

It's something I wanted to pass on to my kids—the discipline, the focus of martial arts. Even with my busy tour and recording schedule, I'd take the time to teach them. We'd go out to the garage, and I'd train them, show them how to punch and kick. I'd quiz them, "What do you do if someone grabs both of your wrists?" My son Mark-Anthony recalls what happened.

> Dad showed my brother and me how to throw somebody if they were to grab our wrists. My brother did the move right away, but I remember sitting in a corner, crying after class. My dad came to me. Got down low on one knee at eye level, and calmly asked, "Why are you crying?"
>
> I said, "I wanted to practice it more. I want to get it right."
>
> So patiently, he lifted me and practiced it exclusively with me, just me. He grabbed my wrists and let me throw his big ole body all over the place. I smiled with satisfaction.
>
> Dad was a black belt, but his approach was always balanced—warm. Serious, playful . . . and no-nonsense.

So now, as I reflect on where I've been and where I still want to go, I find myself asking: "What's next on the horizon?"

Not just for my career—*for me*. I'm still looking for new challenges, new rhythms to master, new terrains to explore. The question is no longer "Can I do it?" but "Do I *want* to?"

I didn't have to stay confined to Hobart Boulevard. That was my starting line, not my limit. And once I realized that, I gave myself permission to *try everything*. Flying. Diving. Martial arts. World travel. Art collecting. Sound engineering. Producing. Learning. Stretching. Becoming.

They're *outlets*. They're acts of exploration. And in my life, exploration is sacred. Because when you grow up in a world that tells you who you're supposed to be, just *trying something new* becomes an act of rebellion. Of liberation. Of *joy*. I do these things not to impress anyone—but to *remind myself that I'm still alive*.

And listen—I don't wait for a group to co-sign what I want to do. I don't need a fan club or a committee. I don't do things for the hype. I do things because they *call me*. I've always been self-directed that way. If I feel something resonate in my spirit, I move. Quietly. Intentionally. And when it's time to shift gears or pick up something new, I don't need permission.

The hardest part of doing anything? Starting. I've said that for years. People want to plan, want to study, want to weigh the options. But most of the time, the obstacle isn't the *task*—it's the *hesitation*. The paralysis of waiting for the right moment.

Let me tell you: The right moment is now. Don't wait for retirement. Don't wait for applause. Don't wait for consensus. Because the truth is, we're only here *once*. And if you're lucky, you find that thing that lights you up from the inside and reminds you who you really are underneath all the titles, achievements, and roles. For me, that pursuit never ends. The next frontier could be thousands of feet in the air—or it could be sitting quietly in a room, writing a new song that speaks to someone I'll never meet.

Either way, I'm still moving forward. Still curious. Still learning. Still climbing. Because life isn't about staying in rhythm with what you've *already done*. It's about daring to discover what still lives *inside you*—waiting to rise.

Chapter 9

Around the World in 80 Earth, Wind & Fire Days

What Earth, Wind & Fire does is so powerful, and I don't mean to be hyperbolic, excited, or enthusiastic . . . I've seen people come into a concert one way and leave another. And it's not because they have been drinking and had a good time, but they had learned something about themselves, and those musicians brought that to them when they were on stage. They find it inside themselves, in each of those performances, within each of those songs, and it pours out and reminds us who we are . . . A sense of brotherhood resonates in their songs and Ralph brings what he does to make it so.

—Sharon Fitzgerald, family, friend, writer

Travel is one of the most significant and transformative byproducts of being a member of Earth, Wind & Fire. It broadened my perspectives; it changed my life. And that wasn't just because I got to see pretty places or taste different foods. It was bigger than that. It was about walking into worlds I had only *imagined*—seeing how others lived, understanding realities far removed from my own, experiencing cultures rich with history, art, and deep nuance.

My first international trip with Earth, Wind & Fire was in 1972, and I still remember it like it was yesterday. Columbia Records President Clive Davis brought us to London, England, to perform at a world convention. That first moment boarding that plane—leaving US soil—my heart was pounding. I was excited, nervous, curious, and exhilarated all at once. We were heading into the unknown. For someone who had spent his life in Los Angeles, that was a revelation.

And when we landed? It felt like electricity.

Everything about London was new—the accents, the pace, the way people interacted with space and culture and history. And because London was our first stop, English was spoken everywhere we went. That made the transition feel a little more comfortable—but it was still like stepping into a *whole other world*.

We stayed at the JW Marriott Grosvenor House, this grand old hotel with a feeling of sophistication and timeless class. I remember being struck by the subtle differences—the way the city breathed, the architecture, the way neighborhoods felt distinct even blocks apart.

While on tour in Europe with Santana in 1975, the legendary Bill Graham walked into our hotel room early and said, "Who wants to go to *Stonehenge*?"

Just like that.

We piled into a bus and rode out across the English countryside to Stonehenge—a prehistoric monument in Salisbury Plain. Those giant vertical stones, some weighing 25 tons, standing like ancient sentinels . . . topped with horizontal lintels in perfect balance. Inside the outer ring stood smaller bluestones. I stood there, looking up at those massive rocks, and my thoughts were full of questions: How did they get here? What did this place mean to the people who built it? Was it a temple? A burial site? An astronomical observatory? I didn't have the answers. But I had a *sense of wonder*—a feeling I carried with me for decades. Someone built this long before us. Someone *came before us.* That realization changed me in a way no record deal ever could.

Then there was Eastern Europe—performing in Germany, in cities like Frankfurt, Stuttgart, and Berlin. The audiences there weren't just polite—they were *devoted.* They knew our songs. They sang along with precision and passion. And to honor them, I'd make it a point to learn phrases in German so I could greet them in their native tongue. I took language lessons in advance, practiced pronunciation, and stepped onstage saying words like *"Danke schön"* with genuine delight. It always earned a smile, and perhaps more importantly—it showed respect.

As incredible as Europe was, it was my return to Japan that captivated me.

Japan has long held a special place in my heart. Before Earth, Wind & Fire became a global force, I was there in 1969 and 1970 with a local band called the Master's Children, playing a club in Tokyo called the Mugen. I was young, unpolished, hungry for experience—and Japan welcomed me into a world both familiar and alien.

Then in 1979, I returned as a professional with Earth, Wind & Fire. That ten-year arc from boy musician to seasoned artist gave the trip a resonance I still can feel when I close my eyes. In Japan, *everything* feels intentional—from the meticulous craftsmanship in their temples to the precision of train schedules, to the way audiences listen *actively*, deeply, respectfully. It was in Japan that I truly understood how music could be received as reverence, not just entertainment.

And tucked inside Yokohama is a personal landmark: the last remaining Tower Records. You remember Tower, right? That's where we all used to go before music got uploaded. Before streaming took the soul out of discovery. I still go there. Still flip through the vinyl. Still chase that feeling.

On a recent visit, I picked up an old pressing of a jazz record I used to listen to as a teenager. I held it in my hands, smelled the cardboard sleeve, and was instantly transported back to Hobart Boulevard, sitting cross-legged on the floor, practicing rudiments, dreaming about playing in front of thousands. It hit me how far I'd come—from that kid with the St. George drum kit to a man playing sold-out shows in Tokyo. That record store is a time capsule, and stepping inside is like shaking hands with my younger self.

Every trip to Japan reminds me why I love what I do. The people. The precision. The peace. We give them our best onstage, and they give it right back. Beat for beat. Smile for smile. Their energy is different—quiet, but strong. Focused. Present. They listen like it matters. Because it does.

And when I look out from the stage and see that sea of faces—polite, prepared, *ready*—I feel an overwhelming gratitude. For the music. For the journey. For the privilege of bringing rhythm to a place that already understands its own so well.

I've always said that each country hears music a little differently. It's cultural, it's generational, it's spiritual. In some places, you play a tune and people jump out of their seats, hands waving, bodies in motion, before you even finish the second bar. In others, they listen with their whole soul—still, reverent, drinking every note like it's sacred. Japan falls squarely into that second category. But *with intensity.* Stillness with voltage underneath.

Every time we played there, the energy was precise. It's hard to explain unless you've stood on a stage in front of 10,000 Japanese fans and tried to keep your heart inside your chest when they all breathe in together on the first chord. And for "Reasons"—man, that song hits different there.

* * *

We were in Tokyo for a sold-out show. Maybe our third night in the city. That particular venue wasn't one of those massive arenas where the sound flies up into the rafters and vanishes. This place had warmth. Beautiful acoustics. Tiered balconies rising like steps toward the stars. Polite clapping before we began. Crisp air outside. Inside, a sea of glowing faces.

We had reached that point in the show that all our audiences, no matter where we were in the world, waited for: "Reasons." Then it started. "Now, I'm craving your body, is this real . . . Temperatures rising . . ." That *first* line always gets them. In Japan, you could feel the whole crowd *exhale*—not in relief, but like they'd been holding their breath for hours just waiting for that moment.

There are nights when a song performs *you*. This was one of those nights. I wasn't playing percussion—I was embracing the moment. My hands knew the song's heartbeat without me having to think about it.

As I looked out over the audience, I saw people mouthing every word. With emotion. With *pronunciation*. That's what always got me about Japan—they *studied* our music. Not just the sound. The intention. They weren't singing along to a hit. They were participating in a shared emotional ritual. "Reasons" was theirs too.

And Phil? Let me say that in the fifty-plus years we've been together, I've seen his vocal range increase dramatically and his command of the stage artistically solidify. Every run, every held note, was a tightrope walk. And he walked it barefoot. But what really made it hit—what made that night *different*—was the quiet. You ever hear 10,000 people hold silence together?

Not fidgeting. Not whispering. Just *listening*. It creates this sonic negative space where every single note matters more. It demands precision. It demands truth. You can't hide behind noise. If you play a wrong note, they hear it. If your timing's off, they *feel* it. And if your heart's not in it? Forget it. They'll know. But that night, we were in sync.

Charles Stepney's arrangement for "Reasons" had always felt like a slow spiral—starting small, then opening outward like petals. It wasn't just a ballad. It was a build. I could feel the chords shifting under my fingers, moving from regret to yearning, from tenderness to pleading. That bridge section—"After the love games have been played, all our illusions were just a parade . . ." always gave me chills. Because you could feel Phil *breaking*. Not vocally—spiritually. It wasn't performance anymore. It was *confession*. It was *soul talk*. And the Japanese crowd heard it that way too. I could *see* it in them—eyes closed, lips trembling. Some couples holding hands tighter. Some just frozen, transfixed.

I remember one woman in the front row—maybe mid-thirties, black scarf wrapped around her hair, tears on her cheeks. She wasn't weeping. She wasn't sobbing. She was just letting the song *wash through* her, quietly. And in that moment, I thought: This is what we were made for. Not the hits. Not the accolades. *This*. This *exchange* between artist and listener where nothing's hidden, and everything's welcome.

That's the power of "Reasons." It breaks through language. Breaks through distance. Breaks through pride. When Phil hit the final lines—those soaring ad-libs over the vamp, stretching each run like silk in the wind—the band pulled back. We *opened up space*. That's the key. You don't crowd him in that moment. You support him. You suspend him. Like holding the edge of a note between your fingertips.

Then the applause came—not as an eruption, but as a *release*. Like the room had been holding its breath and finally remembered how to exhale. Standing ovation. But not wild. *Respectful*. They were saying *thank you*. Not for the song, but for the honesty. Walking offstage that evening, I didn't feel like I'd just finished performing. I felt like I'd just *witnessed* something. That's what it's like when "Reasons" hits right. It's not just a ballad. It's a moment. A memory. A mirror.

I've played that song hundreds of times. But in Japan? That night? It felt like the first time.

For but a brief second, we just looked at each other. And we *knew.*

* * *

We knew—we absolutely knew—that the world was our oyster. When you're part of a band like Earth, Wind & Fire at its peak, that phrase isn't just metaphor. It becomes *reality.* You're not just playing cities—you're being invited into cultures. You're not just filling seats—you're being *celebrated* across continents.

We traveled the globe with open hearts and open eyes, embracing every opportunity to bring our music to people in languages we couldn't speak—but *grooves we could all understand.*

One of the most unforgettable moments of our international touring years was this massive event in London called the Proms in the Park. It was a huge open-air concert in Hyde Park—right in the heart of the city. Tens of thousands of people gathered. Blankets on the grass. Banners waving. The smell of rain and earth and food from vendors wafting through the summer air.

But this wasn't just another show. This was special. We were headlining with the London Philharmonic Orchestra.

A full symphony behind us, taking our arrangements—*our grooves*—and giving them that sweeping, cinematic sound that only strings, brass, and timpani can deliver. The music felt elevated, regal. Songs we'd played a thousand times suddenly felt new, as if we were hearing them for the first time.

And before that concert?

We rehearsed at none other than Abbey Road Studios. The same mixing boards that carried the voices of John, Paul, George, and Ringo. The air in that place feels charged with musical electricity. You walk in and feel the ghosts of genius lingering in every hallway. It is sacred ground for musicians.

And there we were—an American soul-funk band rehearsing with a British orchestra—bridging cultures through rhythm, melody, and mutual respect.

I remember thinking to myself during those rehearsals: *We've really come a long way.* From Chicago to London. From clubs to castles. From dreams to this global celebration of sound.

The concert itself was tremendous. Thousands of people singing, dancing, some crying. The mix of orchestra and Earth, Wind & Fire created something almost spiritual that night. We only did that event once, but it left a mark on me. We had so much fun—so much connection with that audience. I still think about it sometimes. I don't even know if they still have the Proms anymore.

But there was another London venue that became a mainstay for us—and still ranks as one of my all-time favorites: the Royal Albert Hall.

Now *that's* a place steeped in majesty.

The Royal Albert Hall isn't just a venue—it's an experience. The circular architecture. The red velvet seats. The royal insignias. You walk into that place and feel like you've stepped into a painting.

To play there—as an American band, in a foreign country—was no small honor.

That hall has seen classical legends, rock icons, and dignitaries walk through its doors. And when we played there—multiple times over the years—it felt like the building itself *welcomed* us.

The British audience . . . they were different. More reserved than Americans, sure. But *intensely respectful.* Deeply appreciative. You'd see them nodding along, soaking it all in, and then when the groove hit just right, they'd explode with joy—clapping, dancing, even shouting. They understood the musicianship in what we were doing, and that meant the world to us.

There's something incredible about stepping onstage in another country, with another culture, and realizing the music speaks for you. It says everything you can't say in words.

That's what Royal Albert Hall gave us. *A voice* beyond language.

And it wasn't just Europe. We went everywhere.

In the early 1980s, we toured Brazil, one of the most vibrant, alive, soulful places on Earth. We were there off the heels of our *Faces* album, released in 1980.

The crowds in Rio de Janeiro and São Paulo were on another level.

Brazil doesn't just love music—they *live* it.

From the samba in the streets to the bossa nova on balconies to the funk playing in the clubs, it's a part of their national identity. So when we came with our horns, our harmonies, our message of unity and light—they welcomed us like long-lost cousins.

It was hot. Humid. Wild. Beautiful.

At that time, one of their biggest music stars, Djavan, opened for us, and I fell in love with the music and the language. Brazil is a beautiful country with great food, and it is home to some of the most beautiful women I have ever seen. I was selected by the group to sing a verse in Portuguese and address the audience, so I came prepared: "Tudo bem?" I shouted to the crowd. *How are you? Everything well?*

The fans sang along even when they didn't speak English. The percussionists we met were masterful. And the rhythm of Brazil—the heartbeat of that place—got into *us*. You don't leave Brazil the same as you came.

The trip up to the world-famous statue, Christ the Redeemer, is well worth it, along with going to Ipanema Beach. Our photographer, Bruce Talamon, took pictures of the group on a sailing ship. I loved being a water-loving scuba diver, so I was comfortable, but I will never forget the anxiety registered on the faces of Verdine and Maurice, who detested water and boats.

There was one night in São Paulo—I remember it well—we were backstage after a sold-out show. The crowd was still chanting outside the venue. Still singing. That energy pulsed through the walls like electricity. I remember we had cut a side deal that we'd do the show and get a copy, and they would get to keep the sound system. Yes, we left our sound system there in Brazil. We never got that copy of the show, and there was no internet to pull anything from in those days. I've heard diehard fans videotaped it, and it's still swapped among our most faithful.

And I thought to myself, *This is it. Crazy, but this is why we do this.*

Because it's more than travel. It's more than fame. All those years, all those countries, they added something to us. They shaped our sound, broadened our minds, humbled us, stretched us.

But London and Brazil . . . those held something unique. One, majestic and precise. The other, raw and spiritual. Both reminded us that Earth, Wind & Fire wasn't just an American band.

We were global.

We were everybody's band whose music transcended borders.

That's one of the biggest lessons I've learned in more than fifty years of traveling with Earth, Wind & Fire across the globe. No matter what language you speak, what time zone you live in, or what your political history looks like, when the lights go down and the groove hits, the human response is the same. People *feel* it.

And nowhere was that truth more striking than in Russia.

Yes—Russia.

We never imagined, back in the early days, that Earth, Wind & Fire would one day be playing a concert at the Kremlin.

For years, our music was heard across the Eastern Bloc but only in whispers—passed around like sacred contraband. We weren't allowed to perform there back then. Western funk, American soul, spiritual joy—those were considered dangerous exports under Soviet rule. So our sound reached people through *tapes smuggled in, bootlegged albums, clandestine radio broadcasts.*

They *knew* us. They just hadn't *seen* us.

So when that curtain finally opened—and we boarded a flight from Paris to Moscow on March 1, 2005—we didn't fully understand what was waiting for us on the other end.

Two days later, on March 3, we performed at the Kremlin Palace in Moscow.

It was wild. I mean that in the best possible way.

From the moment we stepped onto that stage, you could feel the pent-up energy of a crowd that had been waiting decades to see Earth, Wind & Fire live. It wasn't like a typical tour stop. It felt *emotional.* Like a long-lost family reunion—thousands of strangers who already knew every word, every note, every horn stab and vocal riff.

They screamed. They cried. They clapped on the beat—and off it—but they gave us everything they had.

And we gave it right back.

It's still surreal when I think about it—performing funk and soul in a place that once banned it, standing beneath chandeliers in a concert hall that had echoed with state propaganda not long before.

But on that night? It was music that filled the space.

And then there was Egypt.

We didn't perform there, but that trip left a permanent groove in my memory.

We went as tourists, yes—but also as pilgrims, led by Maurice himself. He wanted to see the pyramids, and when Maurice set his mind to something, we all followed.

We visited the Cairo Museum, full of mummies, masks, and marvels that make your jaw drop. We stood at the foot of the Giza Pyramids, then traveled out to Saqqara, Dahshur, and beyond.

I've been *inside* those pyramids. I've walked the narrow stone corridors built with two million blocks of limestone, stacked by hand, without modern machinery. The sheer mathematical precision, the scale, the *mystery* of how those structures were made—it's staggering.

We stayed at the Mena House Hotel, where you can walk outside and look *straight up* at the Great Pyramid. It took my breath away.

When I look back on it all, I feel this overwhelming sense of gratitude. The travel, the cultures, the stories . . . they've become part of my soul. They taught me that music is not just about performance. It's about connection. It's about being invited into a stranger's world and making it feel like home for two hours under the lights. Traveling the world isn't just one of the perks of being in Earth, Wind & Fire. It's been one of the great honors of my life.

Chapter 10

Honoring a Legacy

Aside from his generosity, my dad is sensitive. People would be surprised that he's a very sensitive person. He doesn't show it outwardly, but he's a very feeling human being. He cares about and is touched by what goes on in the world around him. He's also koach, a word in Hebrew, meaning "having an inner drive that motivates him." You won't see my dad sitting around, riding on yesterday's successes. He's always onto something new.

—John-Ralph Johnson, son, IT specialist

That night at the Kennedy Center Honors, as the song "September" rose to an echoing chant of jubilation, I celebrated with thousands live and a television audience of millions. Yet I was there all by myself, absorbed in my thoughts of how this all came about, what it all meant.

Being honored at the Kennedy Center—that's not just a trophy on the shelf. That's not a "greatest hits" plaque or a fleeting moment of applause. That's something else entirely.

It's an acknowledgment of *choices*—the kind you make in the dark when no one's looking. The kind that aren't always glamorous. The kind that cost you something.

Being there that night, under those golden lights, as a lifetime of sound and memory washed over the room, I thought about those decisions. Not just one or two. But thousands—quiet, unseen, sometimes gut-wrenching, sometimes lonely decisions, made over five decades. All to stay on this path. All to keep the music alive.

There were times—trust me—when walking away seemed like the easy move. There were years when fatigue settled in like fog over the water. When being away from my wife, my kids, my home, started to eat at me. When the hotel rooms all started to look the same. When the creative differences, the business meetings, the long rehearsals, the missed birthdays, the relentless motion of touring and recording—it didn't just wear you out physically. It made you question *everything.*

And there were moments when EWF didn't feel like the dream I had at nineteen. It felt like a machine I didn't recognize.

But I stayed. Not because it was easy. Not because I couldn't do something else. I stayed because I believed in it. Not just in *what we were doing*—but *who we were doing it for.* And because I was proud to be part of something bigger than me. Something that *meant* something to people across generations, across oceans, across languages and cultures.

When I joined Earth, Wind & Fire back in 1971, I had no idea I was stepping into a lifetime. Back then, it was just a tight band with rhythm and fire. Maurice had a blueprint, but none of us could have foreseen the scope of what we were building.

Over time, it grew. And *we* grew with it. I've been with the same musical group for over half a century. That doesn't make me better than anyone. But it does make me *grateful.* And proud. You don't see that kind of commitment much anymore.

How many athletes stay with one team for their whole career? How many professionals retire from the same company they started with? How many spouses hold hands from their wedding day to their final breaths? That kind of loyalty is rare. But it's also *beautiful.* It's not about perfection. God knows we've had disagreements, detours, moments of silence, and seasons of tension. But we never broke. We *bent,* yes. But we stayed aligned. And that matters.

Being honored at the Kennedy Center—sharing that moment with Philip and Verdine and feeling Maurice's spirit humming through the music—I realized that our legacy wasn't just measured in platinum records or Grammy awards. It was measured in consistency. Dedication. Brotherhood. And for me? *Discipline.*

You've got to remember, I wasn't the wild one. I wasn't the loud one. I wasn't chasing the spotlight. I was the one behind the kit, in the groove, staying steady, and later a vocalist up front, but not out front. And in a world that constantly changes, there's value in being the one who *anchors.* My manager, Rhonda Bedikian, shared with me at an awards event once, "*You look at yourself as a soldier to support the group in whatever way you can. Verdine is the real showy one on stage, Phil is the one with the incredible voice, and you, you're the rock."*

Some nights, while everyone else was out partying after a show, I was upstairs stretching, preparing, planning for tomorrow. I was already thinking about the next beat, the next arrangement, the next time we'd have to bring magic to the stage like it was the first time.

I've always approached this as a *craft*, not just a performance. And I've taken pride in that.

That's why the Kennedy Center meant so much to me. Because it wasn't a "fame" award. It was a *contribution* award. It told me, *your effort mattered. Your presence counted. Your faithfulness to the work was seen.*

And when the tribute performance began—when the first chords of "September" rang out across the room—I felt something break open inside me. Not in a sad way. Not even in a nostalgic way. It was like a great exhale. A release.

That song—so joyous, so eternal—rose like an anthem in the hall. People were clapping, smiling, dancing in their seats. It was a celebration. A wave of sound and soul, bouncing off the marble walls of the most prestigious performing arts center in America.

But in the middle of all that noise, I was strangely quiet. I was right there, surrounded by energy, but *deep inside my own thoughts.* And I realized something: I may be in the *September* of my life and career, but I'm *not done yet.*

The Earth, Wind & Fire train that was started back in Chicago? It's still moving. I'm still on board. I still *love* this. I still get goose bumps before the downbeat. I still feel joy when the crowd sings back our lyrics. I still get chills watching a teenager discover "Fantasy" for the first time.

And though the world has changed—the way people listen, the way they consume music, the way they engage with legacy—we've *adapted.* We've *endured.* And we've done it *together.*

I know the day will come when the curtain falls for the last time. That's just life. But let me tell you, *it won't be anytime soon.* Not while there's breath in our lungs and rhythm in our bones. Not while there are still people who show up to sing every lyric, dance in the aisles, and cry through "Reasons." Not while the music still *means something.*

Earth, Wind & Fire will continue until the three of us—me, Verdine, and Philip—look at each other and *agree* it's time to call it. Not when we're tired. Not when the world suggests we should stop. But when *we decide* it's complete.

And when that day comes, we'll step off the stage with grace.

But not yet.

Not while this train still has steam. Not while there's still another city, another crowd, another soul that needs to feel what we've spent a lifetime perfecting.

So yes—being honored at the Kennedy Center meant a lot. But not because it crowned a career. Because it *reflected* one. It reminded me that sticking with something, through the noise and the silence, through the applause and the quiet nights, *means something.* It means everything.

I've been on one team my whole life. And I'm still wearing the jersey.

Because we have endured so long with a level of creativity unmatched by most, we have reaped acknowledgment and awards. The Kennedy Center Honors was just one of the few that really got my attention, but I don't really get hyped up about awards. They're great and all, but you get an award, make your speech, and go home. But sometimes, something sticks out in your mind that made the night memorable. We were awarded a Lifetime Achievement Award from BET at the second annual award show in the summer of 2002. I can't forget that we actually performed our hits at the Kodak Theater in Hollywood and that Steve Harvey and Cedric the Entertainer hosted.

The Rock & Roll Hall of Fame induction in 2000 felt like time standing still—but in the richest sense possible. Not a freeze-frame, not a museum exhibit, but a real, breathing moment that lived and pulsed in the present while it honored the past.

We had all received the call—Earth, Wind & Fire was being inducted as part of the Class of 2000. Being inducted as a member of the Rock & Roll Hall of Fame is a milestone most musicians only dream of. And yet, even in that rare air of honor, none of us truly knew what to *expect*. But when you spend a lifetime carving meaning into sound and spirit, recognition like this isn't about trophies. It's about legacy. That night, they weren't just honoring a band—they were honoring a brotherhood.

Walking into the cavernous hall, the buzz was electric. Lights shimmered off polished floors. Cameras flashed.

There was a sense of history in every corner—plaques, portraits, artifacts, instruments touched by legends. It was a place where time felt both heavy and celebratory.

But nothing compared to the moment when "the nine" walked out onstage together again. And when I say nine, I mean the core members who had literally defined that era of Earth, Wind & Fire—the people who breathed life into the grooves that moved the world:

- Maurice White, whose presence was always with us,
- Verdine White, whose basslines have always been the heartbeat of our sound,
- Philip Bailey, whose voice soared like wind and spirit,
- Larry Dunn, whose keyboard work defined entire textures and moods,
- Al McKay, the rhythm architect,
- Andrew Woolfolk, our very excellent reed player,
- Johnny Graham, with his bluesy guitar overtones,
- And the ever-steady Fred White on drums.

As we took the stage, there was this collective intake of breath that felt like anticipation mixed with relief. Not relief in a nervous way, but the relief of a story finally acknowledged. Of decades of work, creativity, sacrifices, victories, trials—all seen, all recognized.

We each took a moment to say a few words of gratitude—the usual thanks to family, supporters, the fans, the Hall. But deep under those words was something far richer, shared history. You could feel it in the room—not just in the applause, but in the way we looked at each other.

When Larry Dunn and I saw each other on that stage, there was this flash of something—not nostalgia exactly, but something like recognition of a life lived together. To this very day, we remain close and will do for one another whatever is needed.

There's this quiet moment in big events like that—when the chatter fades, and you hear your own breath, and the tick of your heart—and you realize, *this matters.*

There were rumors right away about whether we'd *perform together again beyond that night.* People wanted to see Earth, Wind & Fire back in full, long-form. When nine musicians of that caliber stand side by side, it's only natural for fans, and even friends, to imagine a reunion tour or a full album.

But here's the truth: That night was enough, complete in its own way. We were together, in one place, for one moment—not as a band forced back into motion—but as friends and bandmates who had the rare chance to stand in shared history together.

And then we performed. Not a long set list. Not a marathon comeback. Just the *essentials*—the songs that felt right for that night—"That's the Way of the World," the sound of our purpose; "Shining Star," our song of identity; and I think it was "September," our song of eternal celebration.

The instruments fired up. The amps hummed. The audience rose like a wave—not just with applause, but with emotion.

The energy in that room wasn't just admiration. It was *recognition.* Like they knew, as we did, that those songs had woven themselves into people's lives, into their memories, into birthdays and weddings and graduations and quiet long drives on Sunday afternoons.

From the first note of "That's the Way of the World," you could feel it—decades of resonance, melody, and message colliding in that theater. And when we hit "Shining Star"? Man . . . the way the room lit up, the way the crowd sang back every word—it was like a thousand hearts beating in unison.

Maurice's leadership, his musical spirit, his philosophy filled every note and every breath we took. You could see it in the faces of the guys. In the way Verdine plucked that bassline with authority. In the way Philip's falsetto soared effortless and pure. In the way Larry's fingers painted those keyboard harmonies. In the way Al's guitar lines danced through the air like sunlight.

After the show, we stood together backstage, it felt—peaceful. Not triumphant in the loud sense but settled. Like we had given the universe another layer of witness to the truth of who we were and what we had built.

There was laughter. Handshakes. Old jokes resurfaced and carried on like familiar echoes. People took pictures—not just for fans or media, but for *each other.* Because we were *there.* I remember thinking, *This is what we worked for.* Not the awards. Not the accolades. Not the headlines. But these connections. These moments of mutual recognition.

And when the night came to an end—when the lights dimmed and the suits and dresses drifted toward the exits—we didn't talk about reuniting. We didn't plot a comeback tour. We simply shook hands, hugged, and walked our separate ways *back into the rest of our lives.*

That night was our moment. We were there. We were seen. We were honored. And we were together—one last time on that stage as the nine who helped shape something that *refused to be forgotten.*

And as I walked off that stage—hearing the echoes of applause fade but not truly leave me—I realized something profound: Some reunions are not about revival. They're about remembrance.

Thinking back, one of those nights that stands out—not because of glamour, but because of the *people and the energy*—was the NAACP Image Awards in the fall of 1994 in Los Angeles.

We were on a roll that year. Earth, Wind & Fire had been honored and celebrated in so many ways throughout our career, but the Image Awards carried a different kind of weight—not just for what we'd done, but for who we were as Black artists in a world that had often tried to define our worth for us.

That evening, the atmosphere was charged with warmth and pride. The ceremony was rich with history, culture, and talent. On that same night, we were honored alongside legendary artists like Whitney Houston and Michael Jackson. Just sharing space in the program with their names felt significant. It wasn't about star wattage; it was about recognition from our own community, from people who truly understood what it meant to break barriers and lift spirits through music.

The awards rolled in. I can still remember how surreal it felt when we started getting nominated, back in the early days. At first, it was like a gentle nod from the industry—*we see you*. But over time, the nods became applause, and the applause became standing ovations. And eventually, the standing ovations became awards.

We've won so many over the years, it's sometimes hard to keep track—not because I take them for granted, but because the *work* has always meant more than the recognition.

I've never been one to chase celebrity. I'm not one of those people who walks into a room and scans for the famous or tries to gatecrash the inner circle of Hollywood's elite. For me, it's always been about respect—mutual, grounded, and earnest. When I'm around fellow celebrities, it's usually a quiet acknowledgment: a nod, a handshake, a simple recognition of someone's journey. Nothing flashy. Nothing frantic.

Most of the time, that's enough.

But then there was Ann-Margret. Now *she* was different. To everyone else, she was—and still is—an icon. A true Broadway and Hollywood legend. But for me, she was someone I admired long before fame ever intersected with my own path.

I used to watch her on *The Johnny Carson Show*—laughing, interacting, moving effortlessly between comedy and charisma. She wasn't just beautiful—she was *alive*—genuinely present and utterly comfortable in her own skin. And the way she bantered with Johnny? Man, that was an education in grace under pressure.

A little later, I was in Las Vegas performing—one of those high-energy crowd nights that Vegas does so well—and it happened that Ann-Margret was playing a show at The Orleans Hotel. My good friend Greg Goldstein got my wife and I tickets, so we made a night of it.

Her performance? Electric.

After the show, I had a chance to meet her—really meet her—in those brief backstage moments. She was every bit as vibrant in person as she was on television. Her laugh, her energy, her presence . . . she carried joy and sophistication at the same time. That combination is rare.

We exchanged a few words, talked about *how amazing the audience was*, and shared knowing smiles about the beautiful chaos that is life in show business.

But then something unexpected happened.

What started as a quick hello turned into real, thoughtful conversations.

Later on, I visited her at her home. And when I say *visited*—I mean we sat, talked, and shared for hours.

We talked about life—not the type of shallow chit-chat you exchange at awards shows—but *real life*: art, the inevitability of aging, resilience, spirituality, the things that sustain you when the applause fades. She had wisdom. She had stories. She was curious. She was thoughtful. And she was genuinely interested in what *you* had to say.

Here was this woman—someone I once admired through a screen—and now she was sitting across from me, trading insights about creativity and presence and the nature of being an artist in a world that doesn't always honor depth over spectacle.

She was class personified. I remember thinking how rare it is to encounter someone whose onstage persona matches their real-life presence. Ann-Margret became a special friend—not just a celebrity acquaintance I could check off a list, but someone I genuinely enjoyed talking with as a *facet* of life—interesting, powerful, influential.

I always said I wasn't much of a fan—not in the sense of idol worship. But there are people whose presence *teaches* you something. Ann-Margret was one of those people. Someone I always wanted to meet—and someone who didn't just meet my expectations but exceeded them with her depth, humor, and unguarded authenticity. It's the kind of connection you don't *plan*. It just happens—behind the curtain, offstage, in that space where two artists find resonance not in their *status*, but in their shared humanity.

Still, I'd be lying if I said the acknowledgments weren't meaningful. For the American Music Awards, we won Favorite Soul/R&B Band, Duo or Group in 1980—and that felt *huge* at the time—because the AMAs were always a little more fan-driven. It wasn't about an industry panel or backroom politics. That one came from the people. And for a band like Earth, Wind & Fire—built on connection and love and reaching people where they *live*—that was everything.

We were celebrating our fortieth anniversary and walked away with the Soul Train Legend Award in Atlanta in 2011. That one hit different. When you grow up Black in America, and you come from a community that has always had to fight to be heard, Soul Train is more than a music show—it's a musical movement. It was a platform, a stage that honored us not just as entertainers, but as innovators and cultural leaders.

Then, in 1995, we received a Hollywood Walk of Fame Star that enshrined us in the historical legends of all time. After you get your star, you don't have to explain yourself anymore. They see it daily. Everyone gets it.

And the Grammys? What can I say? There's something about hearing your name called at the Grammys that still makes your chest tighten a bit. You smile. You nod. You try to look cool, but inside, that little kid from South Central LA—the one practicing in the mirror with a hairbrush for a mic—he's flush with pride.

We heard our names called seven times. Seven Grammy Awards. Seven recognitions of being the best at what you do. Each was a milestone. Each one was a snapshot of where we were in our journey:

- Best R&B Vocal Performance by a Duo, Group or Chorus—1975 ("Shining Star")
- Best R&B Performance by a Duo, Group or Chorus—1976 *(All n' All)*
- Best R&B Instrumental Performance—1978 ("Runnin'")
- Best Disco Recording—1978 *(Boogie Wonderland)*

- Best R&B Performance by a Duo or Group with Vocals—1979 ("After the Love Has Gone")
- Best R&B Performance by a Duo or Group with Vocals—1982 ("Wanna Be with You")
- Grammy Lifetime Achievement Award—2016

Each win was meaningful, and each had its own story. I remember being in disbelief when we won for "After the Love Has Gone" in 1979. I knew the track was something special the moment we cut it—the chords, the sentiment, the arrangement—but to see it embraced by the industry at that level, still gives me chills. And then, decades later, came the Grammy Lifetime Achievement Award. That one felt different because it wasn't about a single song or a hit record. It was a recognition of a *life's work* of consistency, of integrity, of endurance. They were telling us: *You didn't just make great music. You made history.*

All the years. All the sweat. The airports. The rehearsals. The sacrifices. The moments of doubt. The high points. The heartbreaks. We had earned this.

But I've never been one to let my reputation rest on a shelf of trophies. My heart is wired for momentum. My joy comes from *creating*, not collecting. That's not ego. That's just how I'm built. Each award is a beautiful moment frozen in time. But life isn't lived in snapshots. It's lived in motion. And my mind is always moving forward—to the next stage, the next song, the next chance to touch a soul or elevate a moment. Because the world *changes*, audiences evolve, and technology shifts. What moved people yesterday may not hit the same tomorrow.

And I've always wanted to be the kind of artist who keeps listening—to the times, to the people, to the pulse of the planet. That's the Earth, Wind & Fire way. That's what Maurice taught us—stay rooted but stay open.

So yes, the awards are meaningful. They are milestones, markers, and reminders of what's been accomplished, but they're not the finish line.

We've still got big plans moving forward. Even after more than five decades on the road, Earth, Wind & Fire keeps the flame burning. We still tour and perform several times a year, and if there's one thing I've learned, it's that the music doesn't retire as long as there are people who *want to hear it.* As long as there are stages to step on and audiences ready to celebrate, we keep showing up.

One of our favorite highlights in recent years has been the New Orleans Jazz and Heritage Festival. We played there in May 2024, and man, that's always a gas. There's something about the spirit of New Orleans that makes music feel alive in ways that go beyond notes and rhythms. The crowds are open, expressive, and deeply connected to every beat. You walk off that stage and feel like you've shared something communal.

But beyond stand-alone festival stops like New Orleans, some of our most requested packages are the ones we've done with the group Chicago. People always ask us to team up with them—and it makes perfect sense. You've got two great horn bands, both with storied catalogs of hits. It's a full night of music when Earth, Wind & Fire and Chicago share the stage. You can sell that show with your eyes closed because people know what a *night like that* delivers—a wall of sound, soaring trumpets, soulful vocals, thunderous rhythms, and arrangements that span generations.

We did that package in 2024, and it was electric. We'd done it three or four times before, but every time feels fresh—like two elder statesmen of music meeting in sonic conversation.

First, both bands usually take the stage together for an opening number. That moment is always fun—seeing all those horns lined up like a parade of brass warriors ready for battle. Then one band steps off as the other takes its turn. Chicago plays a set that highlights their rich rock-meets-jazz sensibilities. Then we come out for our set—funk, soul, gospel-influenced harmonies, and those signature grooves that people have loved for decades.

And then—the best part—we come back together at the end of the night. It's like a celebration in stereo. The whole ensemble onstage, the horns in harmony, the guitars weaving in between, the audience breathing in one rhythm . . . that's a *special moment*. Honestly? That's one of the parts of touring I genuinely *look forward to*—not just performing our own set, but the fusion of two musical families on one stage.

Now, because we had already played together several times, the musical side of the rehearsals isn't complicated. We know the charts, we know the grooves, we know the transitions. The rehearsal time was much more about staging, placement, and choreography—figuring out how we move, where we stand, and how we share the space. That is where Philip takes over—he's great at that. He's the one who says,

"Okay, this is where we start . . . this is where the horn section sits . . . this is when you come in . . . this is when you go there." Because while Chicago tends to stay planted—they're more about *sound than motion*—Earth, Wind & Fire has movement built into the DNA of our performance. We dance. We interact. We *invite* the crowd in with motion as much as music.

One of my favorite moments from those collaborative shows is singing with Robert Lamm—the man who wrote "Does Anybody Really Know What Time It Is?" He handles the verses with that cool, laid-back phrasing, and then I come in on the hook. The blend of our voices—his classic voice from Chicago and my exceedingly cool vocal approach—is a blast to deliver night after night. The crowd always eats that up.

But it's not just the big collaborative packages that give me a sense of fulfillment. Some of my favorite performances don't happen on stadium stages or massive arenas with tens of thousands of screaming fans. Some of the moments I cherish most are in mid-sized halls, venues with soul . . . venues that feel like they *see you back* when you step onstage.

One such place is the Venetian Theatre in Las Vegas—a space that seats about 1,800 people. That theatre is *electric*. It's intimate in the way a great jazz club or a classic Broadway house feels—like everyone in the room is part of the moment, not just a spectator. And that's what makes it special.

Sure—there's the glitz and style that comes with being on the Las Vegas Strip. The lights, the buzz, the glamour that makes the city feel like one long show. But here's the truth, I love the *quiet convenience* of that residency just as much as the performance itself. We've been doing this two-to-three-week residency at the Venetian for four years now.

Here's the beauty of it. You're parked right at the hotel. You walk off the stage, and you don't have to load a bus or race to another city. You just go downstairs. You go play the gig. You go get something to eat right there, maybe one of my favorite Italian restaurants. Maybe you run into a fan in the lobby who tells you how Earth, Wind & Fire songs are their favorites. And then you come back up—your room is two flights away.

That *convenience* changes your life as an artist. It shortens the distance between work and life, between *stage* and *rest.*

And the audience there? They're amazing. Many of them aren't locals. They're people visiting Vegas—on vacation, celebrating anniversaries, birthdays, life milestones—and they *choose* to spend their night with us. Watching all those faces light up—hearing them sing every word—that intimacy is something you don't always get in a stadium packed shoulder-to-shoulder. You *feel* the music in their eyes. You see it in their sway.

I think the Venetian first booked us through our agency—CAA, with our agent Brett Steinberg. They saw something in the pairing of our sound with that audience—something that has proven true year after year.

But over time, something deeper developed. We didn't just do a residency. We built a relationship. Not just between the band and the venue, but between the band and the community of fans who return year after year. People who book their trips around the holidays because their favorite band is playing at the Venetian. Couples who make dinner reservations months in advance. Kids who drag their parents to the show because Mom and Dad danced to our music in college. There's something beautiful about that.

Then, there's the Beacon Theatre in New York City. That place holds around 3,000 people—big enough to feel grand, small enough to feel *connected.* The acoustics are warm. The audience is attentive. It's the kind of room where every note lands right in your chest. We were there in 2024, and it was one of those nights that felt *right.* And then a pleasant surprise happened . . . Hillary Clinton showed up backstage. She remembered when we played at the White House years ago—and she came to tell us, *"Fantastic show. Great to see you all again."*

That's one of those memories you tuck away—not because of the celebrity factor, but because it tells you something about the long arc of your life. You perform one night at the White House, and then decades later, someone still remembers the *feeling* of that moment. Whenever you meet presidents—the Clintons, the Obamas, and they remember you; it's pretty special. It's legacy.

Then came 2025, and with it, another one of those incredible touring highlights—our performances at the legendary Hollywood Bowl.

Now, the Bowl isn't just a venue to me. It's *home.* It's where I grew up listening to music that shaped me. It's where stars have played under the night sky for generations. And when Earth, Wind & Fire gets the call to perform there, especially with an orchestra, it feels like coming full circle.

In the summer of 2025, we returned to the Bowl with the Los Angeles Philharmonic—conducted by the remarkable Thomas Wilkins. This was the fourth time we've played with the Philharmonic there, but this particular run was special for another reason: They filmed a documentary of our performance over two nights—July 3 and July 4, 2025, which also happened to be my birthday. So there I was—celebrating life, music, and family in the place that shaped both.

Verdine wasn't 100 percent during those Hollywood Bowl shows that year. He already knew he wouldn't be able to play the entire set. That was hard for him—because Verdine doesn't *half-step* anything in life. But he made an appearance at the beginning and at the end of the documentary shoot because that's who he is—loyal, committed, and always there for the music and the family.

We brought in an incredible bassist, Ray McKinley, to fill in for the bulk of the performance. Ray has played with legends—Sheila E., Tower of Power, and so many others—and he already *knew the music.* We just had to show him a couple of gestures, place him in the pocket, and he was right there with us.

Watching that performance come together—orchestra and band in sync, the Bowl bathed in light, the audience breathing with the music—reminded me why these dates mean so much. I love the fullness of the orchestra. When strings, horns, woodwinds, percussion, and a living rhythm section lock in—there's a richness to the sound you just don't get anywhere else, and playing the Hollywood Bowl is like performing inside a living sculpture of music and memory.

For us, rehearsals with the Philharmonic are always about the cut-offs, intros, balances, and transitions—making sure the orchestra's voice and our band's voice are one. And because we've done it before, those rehearsals are more about refinement than discovery. We *trust* each other. We *respect* each other. And from there comes magic.

All of these shows—festival stages, packed arenas, collaborative horn packages, philharmonic nights under the stars—they are the continuation of a life's work. They remind me that even after decades, there is still joy in:

- Seeing people sing the lyrics back to us
- Watching older fans relive memories
- Welcoming younger generations who are just discovering our music
- Feeling the collective heartbeat of a crowd when the groove hits

* * *

I will always bask in playing at the Bowl. I can already hear the murmurs of the crowd—people settling into wooden benches, shuffling programs, calling to friends. There's always laughter before an Earth, Wind & Fire show. People arrive early to dine with their wine and cheese, ready to uplift and be uplifted. Our crew moves around with the calm urgency I've known for decades. Drums are checked. Cymbals are polished. The congas, timbales, and bongos have been tuned to perfection. It's time.

Maurice used to say, *"Preparation lets the spirit speak."* That lives in my bones. I don't get nervous. I get present.

The night's set list looks familiar—hits from across eras—but everyone knows the electricity of the night is anchored to one song, the song whose opening guitar line is like a beacon, a song recognizable in fractions of a second: "September." The Bowl is already vibrating with anticipation for it, even before we play a single note.

There's a funny thing about "September." When the writers first worked on it—Maurice, Al McKay, and Allee Willis—the vibe in the studio was instant. That signature three-note intro riff, the smile that hits you before the groove does, the feeling that the song was dancing before we even played it. We knew we'd made something special, but never—not even in the wildest corners of imagination—could any of us have predicted that decades later it'd be a universal language. "Ba-de-ya" needs no translation. So every time I play it, I honor that moment: three creative minds in a room, crafting something that would outlive us all. Which is why, at the Bowl, when I step up on that stage and settle in behind the kit, I'm carrying all of that history with me.

The house lights dim. That familiar, rising roar of the crowd washes over us like surf at the beach. When I walk out, I can feel the Bowl expand—18,000 people leaning in. Our celebrated conductor Thomas Wilkins introduces us, and we walk onstage into that very special Hollywood Bowl night air. Air that is infused with energy and anticipation. 18,000 people, sold out.

We're older than when we started, sure, but when the music hits, age evaporates.

The show eases in with "Sing a Song," "Shining Star," "Got to Get You into My Life"—the stuff that always gets people moving early.

At the Bowl, sound flies differently. The acoustics are legendary, but what amazes me every time is how *alive* the place feels. The roof catches the sound, sends it back, lifts it upward. You can feel the music circulate, almost like the venue is breathing along with us.

As we near the halfway point of the set, we take a moment. We slow things down. Philip sings "Reasons" and the Bowl goes quiet, almost reverent. But everyone knows what's coming. There's a collective, unspoken expectation—we can all feel the gravitational pull toward the last third of the show, where the big ones live. And none is bigger than "September."

Here's a thing most people don't know: Right before "September," there's a kind of sacred silence in my mind. It's not nerves. It's not worry. It's gratitude. I know I'm part of something that has threaded itself into the DNA of joy all over the world. People get married to this song. They dance to it at graduations. They celebrate victories with the song blaring in the background. They heal sadness. They mark time itself—"Do you remember the 21st night of September?" This song carries people. So I honor it every single night.

Al may not always be physically with us onstage anymore, but every guitarist who plays that intro honors his spirit. The guitar intro in "September" is iconic, and when we play it, people come to their feet. This night at the Bowl is no different. I swear, the Hollywood Bowl shakes. Hands go up. Voices spike. Dancers start dancing, even the ones who claimed they wouldn't. The aisles become rivers of movement. Up on stage, I can *feel* that wave lift us. And that's when instinct takes over.

The Bowl lights swirl like a galaxy. And the crowd? They sing the horn lines. Every last one of them. Eighteen thousand people going "BAH-DE YA" You can't help but smile at that. Philip steps to the mic and launches that timeless opening: *Do you remember* . . . And the crowd sings every syllable with him—not behind him, not after him, but *with* him. Perfect unison. Perfect joy. When he reaches the chorus, a chorus he didn't initially embrace, the entire Bowl becomes a choir. *Ba-de-ya! Say do you remember! Ba-de-ya! Dancin' in September*! People wave jackets, cellphones, scarves—anything that catches the lights. I've seen grown men cry during that chorus. I've seen kids barely old enough to talk trying to sing along.

The thing about "ba-de-ya" is that it's pure feeling. No words. No meaning. Just musical sunshine. I watch the joy bloom across the Bowl like a sunrise. It's impossible not to feel it. It's impossible not to be changed by it. From my percussion kit, I can feel the embrace of the orchestra as it sits beneath the iconic Bowl shell. I can see everything: the music rising into the sky; the Bowl arch glowing like a halo; the crowd packed tight in celebration, but above them all—the stars. The Hollywood stars above the Hollywood stars.

And something hits me. We are all part of this moment. Every era of Earth, Wind & Fire. Every fan from the first album to tonight. Every musician who ever dreamed of playing the Bowl. For those five minutes, we're united in the groove.

I lock eyes with Philip, and he smiles that knowing smile—not just a performance smile, but the smile of two men who have lived lifetimes together in rhythm and harmony. Verdine spins around, hair flying, bass thundering, energy bursting out of him like he's plugged into a cosmic socket. He always feeds me energy, always pushes me to dig deeper into the groove. The horns are crisp, punching the night air in perfect three-part harmony. The percussion section beside me is alive—cowbells, congas, shakers, all interlocking. And I am in the center of it.

The groove lifts and the crowd sways. Couples hold each other. Friends drape arms across shoulders. The lights warm to amber, bathing the Bowl in a golden glow.

Time seems to slow. I always take a breath in that moment, soaking in the humanity of it all. In a world that can be heavy, complicated, fractured, here we are—thousands of strangers—singing about love and memory and joy.

Verdine fires the bass. The horns blaze. Philip soars. The Bowl erupts into movement. Everyone jumps. Everyone dances. Everyone sings. I play that last chorus with everything in me—not volume, not force, but intention. The lights spin. The band glows. The night becomes music. We hit the final chord—*BOOM!*—and cut sharply on cue. Silence for half a beat. Then the Bowl erupts. The roar is physical—it pushes against my chest like a warm wave. People are screaming, laughing, hugging. They're glowing.

And in that roar, I hear all the years: the first time we played it. The first time someone told us it changed their life. The first wedding. The first movie soundtrack. The first time a child danced to it with a parent.

* * *

"September" belongs to the world now. All of our work belongs to the world now. *A Grammy Salute to Earth, Wind & Fire Live: The 21st Night of September premiered*, and it was broadcast on September 21, 2025, in honor of our award-winning song. Our guests over those performances included Stevie Wonder, Janelle Monáe, the Jonas Brothers, and Jon Batiste. I was so happy with the way it all came out.

In 2026, a documentary about Earth, Wind & Fire will be released. This isn't just a compilation of old footage or some glossy, half-hearted celebration of a few greatest hits. No, this is something deeper. This is our story, told with care, with respect, and—most importantly—with *truth* by Ahmir "Questlove" Thompson. Drummer. Author. Filmmaker. Historian. A student of the groove. But also, a *caretaker* of culture.

When I heard that Questlove was attached to the project, I felt a quiet reassurance. This wasn't someone looking to cash in on nostalgia. This was a fellow drummer—a *craftsman*—someone who *understood* what it meant to be part of the rhythm section. Someone who knew what it was like to support a sound from the back of the stage, keeping time while the world moves around you. Someone who saw the *whole picture.*

He came to us not with ego, but with respect. He wanted to tell the story right.

It is raw in places. Honest. Surprisingly emotional. There's laughter. There's tension. There are quiet moments where you see what this journey has *cost*. But also moments of triumph—of joy—that remind you why we kept going.

It's a retrospective memoir put to film. Not just of the group, but of the era. Of the culture. Of the movement. Of what EWF meant—not only musically, but spiritually. Socially. Emotionally. It traces our steps all the way from *day one* in Chicago through every stage of the arc—Maurice's vision, the growing pains, the explosions of sound and color in the late '70s, the evolutions through the '80s and '90s, and the resurgence that brought us into the new millennium still standing.

There's so much archival footage in it—things I'd forgotten we even shot. Photos from those first tours where our costumes were handmade and our hotels were humble. Studio clips where you can see the tension and the magic fighting for the same breath. Footage of Maurice writing charts in real time, or Larry hunched over a synth with his headphones halfway off, trying to coax just the right chord voicing out of the keyboard. Snippets of backstage rituals, jokes on the bus, cities we've played that aren't even on the map anymore. And yes—there's current footage, too.

Questlove didn't want to trap the story in the past. He came to *talk to us*. He sat with me for hours, asking thoughtful questions. Not the usual "what was it like" or "what's your favorite show" kind of stuff. He asked about *legacy*. About discipline. About staying. About what it means to give your life to one band, one purpose, one identity—and not run from it when things get complicated.

He wanted to know what it was like to hold down the beat for a group that was constantly moving forward—changing, evolving—and whether it ever felt like the ground was shifting under my feet.

You'll see all of us in the film—Philip, Verdine, myself—speaking in and out of the narrative. Sometimes directly, sometimes woven into voice-overs as the footage plays. Our voices aren't front and center, but they *guide* the story like a rhythm section underneath the melody.

And you'll hear from the people we inspired. That's the part that really humbled me.

Modern artists. Producers. Dancers. Fashion designers. Music historians. Writers. All talking about what EWF meant to them. Not in the abstract, but in their lives. How the music shaped their relationships. Gave them language for emotions they couldn't name. Helped them believe in something when the world around them was telling them otherwise.

We weren't just making music. We were sending out messages—coded in funk, soaked in harmony, built on groove, but carrying something more.

Questlove caught that. He caught all of it: the sweat, the sacrifice, the love. Questlove's film captures the feeling that Earth, Wind & Fire wasn't just a band but a *movement of energy*, built on the belief that music can *heal*, *uplift*, *unite*, and *endure*.

A recent highlight for us was doing Lollapalooza in summer 2025 with the pop star Sabrina Carpenter. She has a monster hit in "Espresso," and I told her if there was ever a hit record, "Espresso" was it.

We were already out on tour, but that show wasn't on our schedule. Our management company got a call from her at the last minute, and they called us to say Sabrina Carpenter wanted us to join her for two songs at Lollapalooza in Chicago. She flew us in—just me and Philip—in her private jet; I think we were in St. Louis. She wanted us to be her guests for two songs of ours she had chosen: "September" and "Let's Groove." We flew in, performed with her, and flew back out. The press coverage and the internet just blew up. It was a great thing.

Earth, Wind & Fire stays busy on the road, but as a band we have not been back in the studio since we received the Kennedy Center Honors. I have been doing some writing and producing, though, and some teaching. My writing has been with Tearce Kizzo, who's from the Netherlands and is a Grammy Award–winning producer for Jon Batiste and others.

Before that, I was in the studio with a group called Funk Asylum and produced a whole album on them. The album is called *Funk Asylum Volume One*; it is a look back at funk and R&B from the '70s, '80s, and '90s. So we did covers of tunes by Rick James, Teena Marie, Shalamar, the Brothers Johnson. During this process, because I was a producer, we had to pick a single. So I'm listening to all this great music and I'm thinking, I'm thinking, and you know, a lot of times when I'm in these situations, I go back and I say, what would Maurice do? And believe me, while I was working on this record, there were times when what I was doing or what I was telling the engineer was Maurice channeling through me. I chose a tune we covered called "I Try," originally recorded by Angela Bofill in 1979. It's a ballad, and ballads are very easy to digest. So far, it's getting a lot of airplay.

My real passion in all this music stuff is teaching. I love to teach. I have two spiritual gifts: teaching and exhortation, or giving advice and counsel. Teaching is important because you have to be able to take care of those who are coming behind you. If you have gained all this knowledge in fifty-some-odd years or however long you've been playing, I think you have a responsibility to teach what you know to others. So teaching for me is the thing, man. I've got drawers of drum books, and I've got two snare drums set up right over here in my studio. I'll have a student come in, and he'll sit on the other snare, and we'll start going through some stuff. I love seeing that light come on. When you lay an idea on them, and they go, "Wow, I never thought about that." That's how you do it. I have been giving drum lessons since 1978 or 1979. One of my former students, music educator Kenny Dickerson, recently told me that I'm the kind of teacher who draws you in and who knows how to take the music off the page and make it accessible for my students.

For me, it isn't work. It's just what I love to do.

EPILOGUE

We're still having fun, and that's why we keep going. I am really looking forward to an upcoming tour with Lionel Richie in 2026. We've been playing with Lionel for several years, and he's such a pleasure to work with. It won't be a grueling tour, just twenty major cities with days' rest in between. That's how we roll now. The difference in touring now for all of us veterans is that it's easier in some ways. It's more organized, and the travel is laid out better. Accommodations are better. Earth, Wind & Fire started driving in station wagons across the country and now travels in airline business class or on private jets. We went from Holiday Inn to Hyatt Regency hotels to suites in the Ritz-Carlton.

But right now, we are still able to smell the roses. It's not in the foreseeable future that Phil, Verdine, or I will be departing. Sure, touring life has its challenges, the toughest being leaving home. I get comfortable being at home. Audiences only see the final product. They don't see that eight-to-ten-hour bus ride that I took in the early morning, or that short nap I took to be up by 1 P.M. to get to the venue and do that 4 P.M. sound check before the two-hour show that night. One can't forget the late-night catering and finally getting into bed well into the next morning so it can start all over again. No one sees that part—the hotel life, the constant travel, the being without your family. One of the most challenging things is gearing up mentally each night, saying, "Here we go. Let's do this for the next couple of hours. Plug in." That's the challenge.

I'm not twenty-five anymore. None of us are. And even though the music still feels good—still moves through me like oxygen—I'm beginning to hear a different rhythm underneath the crowd noise. It's the rhythm of *transition*. The rhythm of *knowing when*.

Because here's the thing. I've already missed so much of my own kids growing up. It's one of the very few personal regrets I carry. That time—those bedtimes, school plays, dinners around the table—it flew by while I was out chasing light and sound around the world.

And I can't go back. But I don't plan to miss my grandkids. That's a line in the sand for me.

I want to be there when they start school. I want to be at the Little League games, the recitals, and the school award nights. I want to be the calm presence in the stands—not FaceTime from backstage.

So, when we had a scheduling call recently—me, Verdine, Phil, and Trinity (Phil's daughter, who helps run our calendar now)—I brought it up again.

It got quiet for a moment.

I think it caught Verdine a little off guard. He's built for this life. He thrives on the grind. He'll keep doing this forever if you let him. That's just who he is. He's tireless. Energizer Bunny–level endurance. He loves it, and more power to him.

But I'm not that guy. I don't need to be here forever. I don't *want* to be here forever. When it's time, it's time.

People talk about *farewell tours*—but the truth is, we don't have a plan. There's no grand finale scheduled. No dramatic sunset farewell.

So, someone's going to have to be the one who finally says it. And that'll probably be me. I'll be the "bad guy." The one who sits the guys down and says, "Hey fellas, I've got one more tour in me. And then I'm out."

That day will come.

And when it does, no one should have any complaints. I've given over fifty years of my life to this one cause. This one family. This one musical vision. I stayed loyal when others walked. I stayed focused when others burned out. I showed up for the rehearsals, the endless flights, the interviews, the late nights, the early mornings.

I stayed. And I gave it everything I had. So when I say I'm ready to go, *I'll mean it.* But here's the thing—That day is not today. Because right now? I'm still finding joy in this. It may not be the same kind of joy as it was in '75, when everything felt like fire and discovery—but it's a seasoned joy. A quiet satisfaction. The real reward now is knowing that we're still bringing something meaningful to people. That people still care. That *the music still matters.*

We gift our audiences with something special, something timeless—and they give it right back in kind. Every time we walk out onstage, whether it's a summer tour, a Vegas residency, or a private performance for a corporate crowd that includes three generations of listeners, the energy is there. And at the end of the night, when we hit that last chord and the crowd rises to their feet and *thanks us*?

That's the moment. Not the money. Not the spotlight. Not the industry applause. It's that moment—when someone in the audience looks up with tears in their eyes and says, *"You made my day better."* That's what keeps me going. That's what makes the flights and the sound checks and the hours of prep worth it—for now. We may be older, but the magic still shows up. And as long as it does, I'll keep showing up, too.

Everything has its season. And I want to leave this stage with grace. With intention. On my own terms. I believe it's important for EWF to be remembered because of our contributions to the social fabric, how we changed how music was recorded, how it sounded, and our approach to our live shows as big productions. As for me, I am satisfied with the amount of fame and fortune I have at this point in my life. It's a trade-off at some point—you have no life once you become so famous. I'm famous enough, whatever that is. How do you even measure that? I don't know. I can still walk outside or be in some social situation, and people may not know who I am. I'm quite happy with that and where I am.

As I stepped out of the Kennedy Center Honors festivities that night in 2019, the cold December air met me like a quiet reminder: *This isn't the end of anything.*

The lights inside were still glowing. You could hear laughter echoing from the marble corridors. The gowns, the tuxedos, the medals—all still shimmering in the afterglow of a night most people only dream of.

And yet, even with all the cameras pointed our way . . . I wasn't thinking about what had *happened.* I was thinking about what's still to *come.* Because my journey? It's not finished. This isn't a farewell. It isn't a swan song. It's a milestone. A beautiful one. A sacred one. But not a final page.

I still have more chapters to live. More grooves to lay down. More notes from this ascending soul to give to the world.

People often ask me: *"Ralph, what more is there to do? What could you possibly add to a life already marked by platinum albums, historic stages, and now, a Kennedy Center Honor?"*

I understand the question. I do. But for someone like me, *success has never been about arrival.* It's always been about evolution. *What's next?* Well—let me tell you.

First, I want to finish my pilot's license. That's been in motion for some time now. Flying has always been a dream of mine—not for the thrill, but for the *discipline.* The structure. The elegance of flight. There's a purity to it. Up there in the air, it's just you, the machine, and the laws of physics. No cheering crowd. No limelight. Just velocity and trust. I've long admired the Blue Angels—not just for their skill, but for their precision, their unity, their show of human potential. To one day fly with them, even once, to fulfill that *military aviation dream* that first lit up my young mind? Man, that would be something. Not for spectacle. Just for the feeling of closing a loop.

I also still have music in me. *More songs in my soul.* You'd think after five decades in Earth, Wind & Fire I might've run out of stories to tell. But no. They've just gotten deeper. More nuanced. There are sounds I haven't shaped yet. Lyrics that haven't arrived, melodies waiting for the right sunrise to call them forward. I know the voice of the world is changing—but I still have something to say in that conversation.

When the time is right, I'd love to revive my record label—on my own terms, with new vision. Not to chase trends, but to *shepherd talent*. To cultivate the kind of musicianship that doesn't just sell but *lasts*. I want to help young artists understand the value of arrangement, of patience, of letting a song *breathe*.

And beyond music? There's a whole other canvas I'm ready to step into. Film. Television. Visual storytelling.

Not from an acting standpoint, but as a producer. An architect behind the curtain. Executive producing stories that carry heart and soul, the way our songs always have. Stories that reflect culture without diluting it. Stories told with edge, with elegance, with *precision*—like a perfectly tuned snare hit or a final cymbal crash.

Cinema is evolving fast, and I plan to stay on the cutting edge of technology. Real-time rendering. Virtual production. Immersive sound design. The same way I watched recording studios move from tape to digital, I'm watching cameras evolve, AI move into storytelling, sound design become part of narrative architecture. I want to be part of that. To *curate* it. To invest in projects that don't just entertain—but endure.

As I walked through the exit that night, the crowd inside still hadn't quieted. The performance of "September" was still *buzzing* in the bones of the building. People weren't leaving.

They were mingling in joy. Hugging. Wiping tears. Sharing memories with strangers as if they were family.

Someone walked up to me as I passed through the crowd. I didn't catch their name. Just the warmth of their hand on my shoulder. "You'll never be forgotten," they said. They meant it as a compliment. But I didn't take it as *past tense.* Because I'm not done yet.

I feel like I'm just entering a new chapter. A kind of creative renaissance. Not louder—but *wider.* I've spent decades mastering one lane. Now, I want to open that lane into a boulevard. I want to mentor. To produce. To direct. To build. Because legacy isn't just about what you've done. It's about what you're *still willing* to give. And for me, I still have *plenty* to give.

So as the lights dimmed behind me and the sound of applause faded into the air, I took one more look at the glowing Kennedy Center. The marble columns, the flags waving gently in the cold breeze, the golden light bouncing off the building like the last note of a perfect chord.

Right now, what I long for most . . . is *home.* Not the tour bus. Not the flashing lights. Not the roar of the crowd or the greenroom chatter before a show. No. What calls to me now are the gentle, unchoreographed moments—the sound of small feet on hardwood floors, the shriek of children's laughter in the backyard, and the unmistakable voice of one of my six grandchildren shouting, "G-Pop!" Or "Pop-Pop!" as I am also called.

That's my name now. Not Ralph. Not my nickname Slick, not just Mr. Johnson or Earth, Wind & Fire's percussionist. These days, I am G-Pop or Pop-Pop—and hearing that, with *joyful urgency*, from a tiny voice that doesn't yet know the weight of the world, is perhaps the greatest sound I've ever heard.

My son, John-Ralph, often tells me, "Dad, anytime my kids are in the car, I make it a point to play Earth, Wind & Fire." He smiles and shakes his head in wonder, like he still can't believe it sometimes. "They know the songs, Dad. They *feel* them. 'Shining Star' comes on, and their little eyes light up."

One of the babies, not even old enough to tie his shoes, throws up his hands like he's conducting an orchestra of stars.

"G-Pop! That's G-Pop!"

They may not understand the lyrics yet, or the legacy behind the music. But somehow, in that raw, honest way that only children can understand, they feel the energy. The joy. The soul. And that's more than enough because *that's* what we were trying to give the world all along.

You know, when I look back at the decades I've spent in this band—in this *brotherhood*, in this *calling*—I realize how much Earth, Wind & Fire taught me. Not just about rhythm and harmony, but about life. About trust. About resilience. About letting go. About holding on.

These are the same life lessons I hope to pass down to my six beautiful grandkids—not through lectures or big speeches, but in the quiet, teachable moments: sitting on the porch at sunset or maybe bouncing on my knee after a grilled cheese sandwich.

I want them to know that dreams matter. That no vision is too far-fetched when you're willing to work and believe. That staying true to yourself is the greatest form of art.

And more than anything, I want them to understand what I've tried to share with *all* of you—those who have listened to our music, sung along to our lyrics, or simply danced in your kitchens to "Let's Groove" or "Fantasy"—pursue your purpose, protect your vision, keep only those in your life who nourish your soul. There are too many people in this world who want to shrink your light. Don't let them. Don't give your energy to anyone who doesn't *see* you. Surround yourself with those who are aligned with where you're going, not just where you've been. And above all, love yourself through the rhythm and through the fire. There is only one *you*. Only one version of your voice, one beating heart that feels the world the way *you* do.

Celebrate that. Protect that.

I've learned that from being in Earth, Wind & Fire. Because, you see, we weren't just a band. We weren't just notes and arrangements and gold records. We were—and *are*—an energy. A timeless force. A reminder that music can uplift, that rhythm can heal, and restore that yearning fire to succeed and be all that you can.

Will there ever be another Earth, Wind & Fire?

No. Just like there will never be another Duke Ellington, another Count Basie, another John Coltrane or Picasso or John F. Kennedy. And I don't say that with ego. I say it with *gratitude*.

We were part of something singular. A rare alignment of talent, timing, and purpose. We weren't perfect men. But we were honest artists. We reached. We stumbled. We climbed again. And together, we helped create a soundtrack for people's lives. And if we did that—if even *one* of our songs got you through a hard day, or made you pull your loved one close on the dance floor, or helped you *believe* when doubt was heavy—then we've done something that matters.

I'd like to think that we were one of those great inspirations, that our sound helped *illuminate* a dark corner. That our joy reminded people to dance even through sorrow.

You know, they say Earth, Wind & Fire music is played somewhere in the world every 98 seconds. Imagine that. Somewhere, right now, a kid is discovering "Let's Groove" for the first time. A grandmother is humming "After the Love Has Gone" in her kitchen. A newlywed couple is swaying to "Devotion." A father is lifting his baby to "September."

That . . . that's the real legacy. The light we sparked in someone's heart.

So if you're reading this—whether you've been with us since 1971 or you just stumbled onto "Boogie Wonderland" last week—*thank you*. Thank you for giving us your ears, your time, your dance floors. Thank you for letting me—a kid from Hobart Boulevard—into your lives. I hope we made your journey just a little brighter. A little more joyful. A little more full of *life*.

Because at the end of the day, this whole experience—the albums, the flights, the performances, the rehearsals, the silence, the laughter, the goodbyes—it all comes down to *this*:

that my grandkids and those close to me get a very candid glimpse of what it was like pursuing my musical dream, the belief, the hope, the humility, the plan.

And for me? That's everything.

That's the final encore.

Thank you.

Thank You

Charley Londoño
Henry Root
Rhonda Bedikian
Kahbran White
Rory Pullens
Henry Carrigan
Ken Rose
Scott Waxman
Evan Phail
Shannon Donnelly
Joann Mignano
John Daniels
Representative Maxine Waters
Roland Martin
Ray Parker Jr.
Kizzo
Siedah Garrett
John Clayton
Howard Hewett
Stephen Quadros
Reggie Calloway
Smokey Robinson
Special thank-you to Questlove

Song Permissions

“After the Love Has Gone” By Bill Champlin, David Foster, and Jay Gradon. Copyright © 1978, 1979 EMI Blackwood Music Inc., Peer Music, Music Sales Corporation (ASCAP), Foster Frees Music, Inc., Garden Rake Music, Inc., and New Music Inc. All rights on behalf of EMI Blackwood Music Inc., Foster Frees Music Inc., Garden Rake Music Inc., administered by Peer Music & Sony Music Publishing, (US) LLC, 1005 17th Avenue South, Suite 800, Nashville, TN, 37212. All rights reserved. Used by permission.

“Boogie Wonderland” © 1979 EMI April Music Inc., EMI Blackwood Music Inc., & Universal Music Group. All rights on behalf of EMI April Music Inc. & EMI Blackwood Music Inc. administered by Sony Music Publishing (US) LLC, 1005 17th Avenue South, Suite 800, Nashville, TN, 37212. All rights reserved. Used by permission.

“Fantasy” © 1977 EMI April Music Inc. & Criga Music. All rights on behalf of EMI April Music Inc. & Criga Music administered by Sony Music Publishing (US) LLC, 1005

17th Avenue South, Suite 800, Nashville, TN, 37212. All rights reserved. Used by permission.

"On Your Face" By Philip Bailey, Charles Stepney, and Maurice White. Copyright ©1976 by Saggifire Music /EMI Apil Music (ASCAP) and Embassy Music Corporation (BMI) International Copyright Secured. All Rights Reserved. Used by permission. All rights on behalf of EMI April Music Inc. administered by Sony Music Publishing (US) LLC, 1005 17th Avenue South, Suite 800, Nashville, TN, 37212. All rights reserved. Used by permission.

"Reasons" By Philip Bailey, Charles Stepney and Maurice White. Copyright © 1975 by Saggifire Music /EMI April Music (ASCAP) and Embassy Music Corporation (BMI) International Copyright Secured. All Rights Reserved. Used by permission. All rights on behalf of EMI April Music Inc. administered by Sony Music Publishing (US) LLC, 1005 17th Avenue South, Suite 800, Nashville, TN, 37212. All rights reserved. Used by permission.

"September" © 1978 EMI Blackwood Music Inc., EMI April Music Inc., Steel Chest Music, Universal Music Group. All rights on behalf of EMI Blackwood Music Inc., EMI April Music Inc., Steel Chest Music administered by Sony Music Publishing (US) LLC, 1005 17th Avenue South, Suite 800, Nashville, TN, 37212. All rights reserved. Used by permission.

About the Author

Ralph Johnson is the percussionist and vocalist for the legendary band Earth, Wind & Fire. As an original member, he has witnessed five decades of thrills and awards including ASCAP, NAACP, and BET; Rock & Roll Hall of Fame induction; a star on the Hollywood Walk of Fame; Kennedy Center Honors; and eight number one hits, leading to seven Grammys and a hundred million albums sold globally.

Rory Pullens is currently the chief learning officer for Soapbox LLC. He was a Hollywood scriptwriter/editor and content creative. A prominent national leader in arts and music education, Pullens has led organizations in Los Angeles, CA; Washington, DC; and Denver, CO.